Psychoanalytic Insights into Fundamentalism and Conviction

Psychoanalytic Insights into Fundamentalism and Conviction: The Certainty Principle examines the role of, and need for, certainty in mental life, addressing questions raised by fundamentalism and extremism and exploring its relation to human nature. Murdin proposes a new synthesis in which certainty itself can be a cause of suffering and part of a defensive manoeuvre, and considers how the need for certainty can be managed in a positive way, rather than creating fear and extreme emotional responses.

Illustrated throughout with examples from psychotherapy practice, literature and international politics, this book considers how the quest for certainty dominates much of human thinking. Murdin examines personal relationships, including politics and religion, where assumptions are taken for granted but function to hide fears and doubts, and argues that fundamentalist elements can generate harm in anyone but can be mitigated with understanding and work in therapy.

Psychoanalytic Insights into Fundamentalism and Conviction helps to identify the underlying convictions that are causing mental harm. It is essential reading for psychotherapists, psychoanalysts and counsellors in practice and in training, and will be of interest to readers interested in fundamentalist states of mind.

Lesley Murdin is a psychotherapist with a private practice in Cambridge, UK, and was formerly the National Director for WPF Therapy in London. She has worked at the UK Council for Psychotherapy and the British Psychoanalytic Council to develop professional standards, and is the author of several books, including *Managing Difficult Endings in Psychotherapy, Setting Out: The Importance of the Beginning in Psychotherapy and Counselling* and *How Money Talks* (all Routledge).

Psychoanalytic Insights into Fundamentalism and Conviction

The Certainty Principle

Lesley Murdin

Routledge
Taylor & Francis Group

LONDON AND NEW YORK

First published 2021
by Routledge
2 Park Square, Milton Park, Abingdon, Oxon OX14 4RN

and by Routledge
52 Vanderbilt Avenue, New York, NY 10017

Routledge is an imprint of the Taylor & Francis Group, an informa business

© 2021 Lesley Murdin

British Library Cataloguing-in-Publication Data
A catalogue record for this book is available from the British Library

Library of Congress Cataloging-in-Publication Data
Names: Murdin, Lesley, author.
Title: Psychoanalytic insights into fundamentalism and conviction: the certainty principle/Lesley Murdin.
Description: Milton Park, Abingdon, Oxon; New York, NY: Routledge, 2020. | Includes bibliographical references and index.
Identifiers: LCCN 2020008418 | ISBN 9781138362161 (hardback) | ISBN 9781138362178 (paperback) | ISBN 9780429432255 (ebook)
Subjects: LCSH: Belief and doubt. | Certainty—Psychological aspects. | Radicalism—Psychological aspects.
Classification: LCC BF773 .M87 2020 | DDC 153.4–dc23
LC record available at https://lccn.loc.gov/2020008418

ISBN: 978-1-138-36216-1 (hbk)
ISBN: 978-1-138-36217-8 (pbk)
ISBN: 978-0-429-43225-5 (ebk)

Typeset in Times New Roman
by Swales & Willis, Exeter, Devon, UK

Contents

Acknowledgements

My thanks go first and last to my husband Paul Murdin who has helped and supported me in the whole process of writing, but particularly in reading and correcting the manuscript.

I also want to thank Celia Harding for her thoughtful help with clarifying my thinking and offering me valuable references.

I am grateful to Andrew Samuels and Heward Wilkinson for support in undertaking the project.

For reading chapters and giving me valuable feedback I thank Jane James, Sophie Pierce and Patricia Pinn. For useful references to psychological research my thanks go to Francesca Handscombe. Lastly, for the cover design my thanks go to Alexander Murdin.

Preface

This book has been written at a time of political uncertainty and accompanying tension all over the world. Climate change and the problems that it brings for all of us are never far away from the individual or the Consulting room. Populism means that the old consensus of the power of the educated elite has faded away and no-one knows where we go from here.

There has been much emphasis on the fundamentalism that leads to terrorism but there is also a strong body of opinion led by such people as Sayeeda Warsi in the United Kingdom arguing that we must not attach the responsibility for terrorism any one group. She argues that we must not assume that strongly held religious belief or cultural practice equates to terrorism. I hope that this book will contribute something to the argument that fundamentalism, in the sense of beliefs that are passionately defended in the face of every argument or piece of evidence to the contrary, can be harmful in many ways even if not realised in violent action. In this debate I completely accept that no one religion or culture is responsible for violent action but I also look at the forces in society and in the individual mind that can lead to destructive behaviour, whether that is physical or emotional.

For this purpose I have looked at the main areas of personal and social life to see where, how and why we are afflicted with unwarranted certainties. I have argued that some of the most damaging convictions are those that are not even consciously known to their owner but have persisted from long ago or even from childhood. I have looked at personal relationships, politics, religion and some of the areas of mental distress that are common in our society. In each case I have found beliefs that are harmful. I have tried to find some understanding of the place of doubt and certainty in each area and in looking at it from the point of view of a therapist have moved on to consider how change can come about.

I have written this book in the hope that it will help people to think about the importance and value of doubt and questioning as well as the need for conviction in its proper place. What is its proper place? That is one of the matters that I hope to consider here so that we can all weigh up evidence and decide for ourselves. Above all, I hope that the book shows the value of a questioning and thoughtful response to what our leaders and authorities tell us.

Terminology

I use the term 'patient', which means literally 'the one who suffers', and not 'client', which means 'dependent'.

To avoid speaking uniquely to any one group I use the term 'therapist' to include counsellors, psychanalysts and psychotherapists. Not all do valuable work but they all can be harmful if they are too sure that they are right.

I am not very passionate about pronouns but tend to use the feminine for the therapist and the masculine for the patient just to make a helpful distinction.

Chapter 1

Certainty
Who needs it?

> The best lack all conviction, while the worst are full
> of passionate intensity.
>> W. B. Yeats, 'The Second Coming', 1919

The Irish poet W. B. Yeats wrote 'The Second Coming' in the aftermath of
the First World War and in the context of the Irish War of Independence.
He pointed out the disjunction that we find between those whose certainty
is supporting destructive positions and those whose doubt is part of their
ability to see the complexity of life's choices. Much of the distress in living
arises from a failure to find the middle ground.

Marianne commutes to a job in London through the major UK train
station Kings Cross. She tells me that she enjoys commuting. Mostly. It
gives her time to think and often she reads a novel on the train. 'But', she
says, 'I dread the bit in the station. I look round all the time for the man
with the gun but I'm also expecting a new kind of attack, maybe gas or
a bomb'.

Perhaps Marianne will get used to the fear and become less anxious.
Perhaps her anxiety will shift to something closer to her and to what she is
doing or is about to do. Ellie on the other hand tells me that she never
thinks about danger. She has decided just to get on with her life. She will
not allow herself to think about what might happen. 'Well', she says, 'you
can't live like that. You have to think it won't happen to you'. Without
meaning to, she shows that she is well aware of her fear but she can usually
chase it away from her mind, replacing it with certainty that she will be all
right.

Both of these women have been affected by the damaging certainties of
others that we might group under the heading of 'fundamentalism'.
Whether or not there is a high risk of terrorism in a given place at a given
time, there is a tension in the human mind between doubt and certainty.
Both are needed but both can be problematic. This book is an attempt to
consider some of the areas in which these states of mind show themselves

and to look at how and why people are able to change their minds. Fundamentalism is not limited to religion or politics but is part of every person's mind-set. I will also consider the need for therapists to be able to see that there are different ways of approaching a person seeking help and that there may be wrong ways but there is very unlikely to be a right way that provides certainty.

People want to feel safe and secure. There are dangers both in people's own minds and in the outside world. Of course, terrorism is a special case and this book will be much more concerned with the internal fears and anxieties of each individual. Yet it is also true that our environment presents us with physical and emotional dangers every day.

As a psychotherapist, I hear about people's hopes and also about their fears. I know that everyone has their own versions of both but I am aware of some social as well as psychological conditions that lead more to fear than hope. Some people are able to overcome fear about the dangers in the environment enough to shrug them off. Older people might look back with some nostalgia to days when the greatest danger in big cities was a mugging by criminals. Since 9/11 (the attack on the Twin Towers of the World Trade Center in New York in 2001) and other terrorist attacks elsewhere in the world, the fears are more cataclysmic and are based on known history. This is one reason for spending some time thinking about the nature and development of fundamentalism in our environment. When we look at it closely, we can see that there is something fundamentalist in all of us. The psychotherapist needs to see the difficulties of that. Since convictions that defy the facts of experience are likely to be shored up with all kinds of defences, she will need to help people to look honestly at what they believe to be true.

What is fundamentalism?

In fact, fundamentalism is a solution to the problem raised by the doubt and uncertainty of ordinary life. Since fear is predominantly aroused by the unknown and the unpredictable, we try to establish certainties at two levels. At one level we have the convictions of each individual: 'One thing I know is that I will never be able to speak Chinese fluently. It just isn't me'.

We also create certainties for ourselves in terms of social threats. This might be one place where terrorism provides a contemporary illustration. By seeking out the perpetrators and removing them, political leaders seek to convince populations that they will be safe in the future. In addition to political persuasion there is some truth in the saying, 'There is safety in numbers'. Watching a school of small fish or a flock of birds, you can see that a predator might be so confused that he catches nothing but, in any case, the chances of being the one caught are much less than for a solitary fish or bird. Human beings cling together with shared beliefs but for the bonding to hold, they must all be certain of their common beliefs.

One definition of fundamentalism is 'strict adherence to traditional orthodox tenets'. In order to 'adhere strictly' to tenets of belief, it is necessary to be certain of what those tenets are. The ardent fundamentalist cannot allow any doubts to arise. He knows that it is only for as long as he believes that he can belong to the brotherhood of fellow believers. Needing to belong to a group nourishes fundamentalism but this book will also consider other reasons for the need for certainty.

Beginning with fundamentalism as a social phenomenon I will show that the need for certainty is at work in the reaction to the terrorist attacks on New York and London. This is not to say that all fundamentalism leads to terrorism but that the mind-set involved also appears in individuals and can lead them to damage themselves and others.

Fundamentalist action begets response in kind

One view of the terrorist attacks of 2001 and 2007 is that they were caused by religious extremism. Some of the preachers of Islam not only pointed out the decadence of Western society but also urged that it was morally virtuous to seek to destroy it. Young people seeking to assert their strength and their virtue were given a task which would excite and test them and would lead to rewards in heaven. Other views might consider the part played by envy and desire for a share in the wealth of Western societies. Mohsin Hamid shows these more hidden forces at work in his novel *The Reluctant Fundamentalist* (2007), which I will consider in detail later.

Once these forces are released, the attacked can become the attacker and both in talion law, the principle that someone who has injured another person is to be penalised to a similar degree – 'an eye for an eye', believe that they are entitled to revenge and to inflict as much harm as they can. A cycle of violence builds up with more and more powerful conviction of being right on each side.

Since the attack on the Twin Towers, the phenomena of fundamentalism have been discussed in media of all sorts in the English-speaking world. Terrorist attacks elsewhere have sparked similar discussions in the world at large. To understand the processes at work we need to look at the particular rewards that are evidently gathered by those who are involved.

Why do people seek certainty? Dangerous external events echo dangers in the mind. Conviction will provide safety. Knowledge can be a gateway to this felt need but so can all sorts of dubious, unfounded beliefs. Factual information provides a sense of control. We are helpless while waiting to see whether the man on a train fiddling with his backpack is really about to set off a bomb. But there might be some information about the profile of recent attackers that would help to allay anxiety. There might still be some doubt but knowledge might change the weight of probability from conviction of danger to a shrug that says that this is probably not dangerous.

As a result of these sorts of experiences in the social consciousness, governments have begun to take an interest in the pattern of thought that can be considered to be a 'passionate conviction'. One approach that writers have taken is to examine the nature of fundamentalism as the root of problems of violence and consequent fear. Overt violence is one manifestation of conviction but much that goes on in the individual is hate and anger, which also arise from some of the same sources. The social and the individual merge in this area and some of the same psychological patterns can be seen in each.

The attraction of fundamentalist mind-sets

There are difficulties in writing about fundamentalism because of the multiplicity of definitions available. There are dictionary definitions, commonsense definitions and, less commonly used, psychoanalytic definitions. Dictionary definitions like the one quoted above emphasise strict adherence to a set of beliefs, which are often religious or acquire a religious force. The term 'fundamentalism' originates from a set of books published in the early twentieth century called *The Fundamentals*, resisting the influence of modernism by advocating a return to the founding beliefs of Protestantism (Summers 2006: 329). These definitions often emphasise rigidity, and hostility to any challenge. Hostility is aroused in part by fear of those who might not share the same conviction. Like an animal encountering a stranger in its territory, a person in this position may turn, with violence, against those who are not members of the circle of believers.

Belonging is one of the main motivators of human beings. The extraordinary power of social media to involve people and fire up emotional responses is connected to the wish to be part of a group. The evolutionary value of this is clear. From primitive societies onwards it has been necessary to form groups, to hunt and eat and to be protected from predators and hostile human beings. At the macro level we need to belong to a group and at the individual level, the human infant must belong to a mother. She must accept him feed him and care for him so that he can survive.

While the story of human development shows us some reasons for a need for certainty, there are many other reasons at both social and individual levels.

In his examination of gullibility, *Factfulness* (2018), Hans Rosling considered the way in which beliefs are formed and maintained in the face of contrary evidence. He posed questions about matters of fact to many different audiences throughout the world and found that on a typical question about the prevalence of poverty, vaccination rates or literacy rates for girls and women, audiences gave wrong answers with staggering frequency. Rosling pointed out that if he brought along a pile of bananas to a group of chimpanzees, labelled the bananas and asked the chimpanzees to answer his questions by picking a banana labelled *a*, *b*, *c* or *d* — in other words, he generated completely random answers — he would get correct answers more frequently than from the most educated audiences in Europe. He then set out to explain this strangely inaccurate world view held stubbornly even in the face of evidence by so many people.

Rosling's conclusion was that we like drama. Stories have fascinated people as far back as history can take us:

> It is the overdramatic world-view that draws people to the most dramatic and negative answers to my fact questions. People constantly and intuitively refer to their worldview when thinking, guessing or learning about the world. So if your worldview is wrong then you will systematically make wrong guesses.
>
> (2018: 13)

He sees this as evolutionarily valuable: 'We are interested in gossip and dramatic stories which used to be the only source of news and useful information' (2018: 14). Of course, our ancestors would pay attention to an alarm call. Mothers are all still alert for the snake that will catch their babies or the leopard that will grab the weakest. Rosling sets out to show how a desire for the dramatic story can blind all of us to the truth, which may be simple or even boring. If we are hard-wired to listen for the dangerous but exciting news, we will reject that message as untrue only after a struggle. People seeking therapy may have the same blindness to their own truth and we can help ourselves, and each other, by watching for the signs of misinterpreting.

Love of drama and excitement are not the only motivation that leads to baseless conviction. Belonging is also vital to a tribal animal. In order to belong to a circle of believers you must meet the requirement of being absolutely certain that you are right. The group itself will help to reinforce the belief. The knowledge that others share the conviction will help to maintain the belief. In considering this, we can see that certainty arises from a desire to belong to a group and that this causes trouble in many areas of human life.

This might be considered a view of motivation based on social psychology. Psychoanalysis offers much else for consideration when we ask why people cling to beliefs. One area of thought concerns the superego. Most of us very much like to be right and find it humbling to say 'I was wrong'. The nature and structure of this agency in the mind was examined from different angles in Celia Harding's wide-ranging collection of papers on the superego (2019). She points out that the child is inclined to overestimate her own strength and ability and unless this is modified in a loving and supportive environment, disillusionment will lead to a harsh and rigid view of the self. Aggression and hate are linked to the defence of the threatened part of the self. We see the effects in much of public life. Quite apart from risking law suits, most politicians hate to say that they are sorry about any past actions. In such a position there can be no satisfactory changing of one's mind (2019: 80).

Warren Coleman, in the same book, points out the importance of the ego ideal: that view of the self that we all hold and often hide in order to link to the beauty and strength of those we admire (2019: 173). Therapists usually have trouble with their superego and their ego ideal which, as Coleman points out, can lead them into levels of conviction and self-attack that cannot usually be helpful to their patients. Recognition of the action of this part of the mind is vital both for the therapist's own wellbeing and that of her patients. The problem that then arises is how can any of us be helped to modify the action of the superego so that it is not just looping between a set of fundamentalist beliefs and a sense of failure in not being able to live up to them.

Assessing belief

Being able to think about the past and the future enables the human mind to estimate the value of information and to assess its level of certainty. The scientific method of observation and experiment provides a template for assessing the accuracy of any statement or belief. What we then find is that there is a longing for certainty, which most aspects of life cannot supply. We see the level of psychotic functioning entering the demand for certainty. The wish that this would be true might be enough to convince that it is true. What might be the causes and the effects of this longing will form one of the questions to be investigated in this book. The investigation will then enable consideration of how the wish for certainty can be mitigated in a way that prevents harm from being done to the individual and to those around him.

A case study of damage from conviction

When the Twin Towers of the World Trade Center in New York were destroyed in 2001, we can see that one of the main difficulties for Americans, as expressed by President George W. Bush, was that they had lost the certainty that the United States were invulnerable. From then on, the belief that no-one could attack Americans on their home soil was shattered and the new world that had to be faced demanded that everyone should recognise that they are vulnerable. Bush rushed into action as soon as he could.

He wanted to be certain about who the enemy was. The principle of talion law allows revenge to take the same form as the original crime and therefore can involve violence and destruction. If the enemy were identified convincingly they could be hunted down and destroyed.

The Federal Bureau of Investigation was very soon able to identify the 19 men who had boarded the planes that crashed into the Twin Towers because they left records of passports and other documents behind. In some cases, passports were found whole in the wreckage. In other cases, passengers and staff on the planes had telephoned with descriptions of the hijackers before they all died.

Those who lived through the experience of 9/11 knew that the enemy was very soon identified with no room left for doubt. Because of the work of the FBI, names were available as well as the general belief that it was an organisation calling itself Al Qaida that devised and carried out this plan. The emotional level surrounding the event was increased by the news media, which, for example, showed people jumping from the burning buildings and played tapes of the last messages from people on the planes. The impact on many people was a willingness to accept the guilt of the 19 men and then to join a wish to catch and punish those who had instructed and enabled them. This was orchestrated and nurtured by the mass media. For many, perhaps most, reading about 9/11 in the papers or seeing it on television or on social media is enough to convince. The desire to believe a particular story is also very powerful.

Records of the President's behaviour at the primary school where he first heard the news and after that on board his plane, Air Force One, show that he was shocked but more than that, he was very angry. His subsequent behaviour shows the power of the fusion of anger with passionate conviction. He spoke of 'those bastards' and promised to find them and hunt them down. He has since been accused of going for accessible targets in the invasions of Iraq and Afghanistan rather than waiting so that he could fight those who had supported and presumably financed the perpetrators. We can see that he desperately needed to replace the old certainty with a new certainty about an enemy that could be attacked and visibly damaged. One certainty was destroyed and the response had to include a replacement.

Of course, everyone chose their certainties according to their own belief system. For example, Jerry Falwell, the American television evangelist in the Christian Broadcasting Network's TV program, *The 700 Club*, called the event a punishment from God. He said,

> I really believe that the pagans, and the abortionists, and the feminists, and the gays and the lesbians who are actively trying to make that an alternative lifestyle, ... all of them who have tried to secularise America, I point the finger in their face and say, 'You helped this happen'.
>
> (Laurie Goodstein, *New York Times*)

According to a spokesman commenting on Falwell's remarks, 'the President believes that terrorists are responsible for these acts'. Falwell issued a statement agreeing with this and apologised for his previous comments (Goodstein 2001).

War is very certain

Bush focused on creating a new narrative for people to accept and cling to. He named this the 'war on terror'. The term covered a great deal of activity in the United States and across the world. This demonstrated the power of short memorable slogans to construct a new reality. Bush wanted the world to agree that as the leader of Al Qaida, Osama bin Laden had become the enemy who was named and whose death would free the world from terror.

The facts defining the role of bin Laden in the terror attacks are difficult to assess. There was considerable confusion over the extent of bin Laden's personal involvement in the attacks. He claimed prior involvement but not direct responsibility. On the other hand, he never distanced himself in any way at all. In fact, a threatening message from bin Laden which was read by Sulaiman Abu Ghaith, a spokesman for Al Qaida, on the Al Jazeera TV network in 2001 ensured his place as the Enemy and ultimately sealed his own fate:

> The Americans should know that the storm of plane attacks will not abate, with God's permission. There are thousands of the Islamic nations' youths who are eager to die just as the Americans are eager to live.
>
> (BBC Monitoring 2001)

As we know, the response from the Americans was to invade Iraq and Afghanistan, with far-reaching consequences for many people. The certainties that made this possible have long since faded. Yet, ten years later, President Obama ordered his Navy Seals to raid the house in Pakistan where bin Laden was hiding, with authority to kill him. There was no uncertainty about bin Laden's guilt, or what was effectively his execution. But even in this state of certainty there was controversy about the official account of the raid, in particular over the role of Pakistan in bin Laden's concealment (Mahler 2015).

Doubt and fear can create certainty

Looking at these events helps us to see some of the human responses to fear and to the ways in which we seek a narrative and a structure. Judging by the UK media, most people accepted that the death of bin Laden was the end of a terrible story. Justice had been done and we could sleep more soundly. On the other hand, events had damaged the belief that bad things happened only in the Middle East and not in Europe or the United States. Subsequent attacks have left us all liable to be as frightened as Marianne who was mentioned at the beginning of this chapter.

The ghastly image of collapsing towers, which had been fixed in our collective minds for years, was to some extent displaced by the image of President Obama and his senior advisers huddled tensely around a table in the White House Situation Room, watching closely as justice was finally brought to the perpetrator. The potency destroyed in the collapse was restored for Western society at least for a time.

Finding the culprit in a specific crime involves intensive analysis of data. People expect the investigators to find and punish the guilty parties. In the major disaster of the Twin Towers, we seem to accept that justice was done. In other more diffuse questions, we can be very reluctant to believe the evidence.

No time to wait: this must be right

One of the factors leading to unwarranted certainty is impatience. President Bush was in a great hurry to find the culprits of 9/11 and as such he seemed to have found his answer quickly. Nevertheless, journalists have proposed conspiracy theories that say that the whole story of the raid on bin Laden's enclosure is unbelievable:

> [F]alse stories couldn't have reached the public without the help of the media. Reporters don't just find facts; they look for narratives. And an appealing narrative can exert a powerful gravitational pull that winds up bending facts in its direction.

> (Mahler 2015)

Rosling points out that there is advantage to being able to decide quickly what to do. When the leopard leaps out of the bushes there is no time to analyse:

> We are the offspring of those who decided and acted quickly with insufficient information ... the urgency instinct can also lead us astray when it comes to our understanding of the world around us.

> (Rosling 2018: 227)

The perceived need to act urgently encourages the formation of unwarranted certainties. 'If I don't act now, I will lose the opportunity for ever'. So I have to believe that it is right to act and I become certain. Rosling points out that over-dramatisation of what we know can lead either to overreaction without analysis or to giving up and equally not analysing the evidence.

Drama is something we all seem to enjoy. Maybe it is better named as a love of narrative or of story. That is a need for shape and meaning in a life that is often filled with events that do not make sense and so do not have a satisfying meaning. The need for control is also implicated to some extent in the shaping of a narrative. One way in which we shape events into something that makes sense is through finding a conspiracy, putting someone else's meaning into what does not otherwise make sense.

Maintaining belief: what can we take to be evidence?

We know about conspiracy theories since, for example, the media told us about the forged Hitler Diaries, which in 1983 were authenticated by the historian Hugh Trevor-Roper (although he later withdrew his endorsement). They turned out to be an elaborate forgery by a man called Konrad Kujau (Hamilton 1991). Brian MacArthur (1991) emphasised one of the problems of certainty: once a person has affirmed a theory especially in public most people find it very hard to abandon it:

> The discovery of the Hitler diaries offered so tempting a scoop that we all wanted to believe they were genuine. Once hoist with a deal, moreover, we had to go on believing in their authenticity until they were convincingly demonstrated as forgeries ... The few of us who were in on the secret fed on the adrenalin: we were going to write the most stunning scoop of our careers.
>
> (MacArthur 1991)

The language of certainty in public and private domains

The language that we have available to us determines what we can think. This is a sweeping statement but has been proposed by philosophers such as Whorf (1956) and refuted by more recent writers such as Stephen Pinker (1994) on the grounds that thought is not based on any language. Whatever the outcome of this debate, words and phrases get caught up in the psyche and do exercise considerable power over thoughts and actions.

The language of political certainties

At the beginning of the twenty-first century a popular phrase used by the President of the United States in his nocturnal messages on Twitter is 'fake news', which implies that deception goes on and is rapidly spread by social media. Social media are very good at spreading 'news' whether it is true or not. Conspiracy theories such as holocaust denial or the various narratives about the death of American President John Kennedy or the 9/11 bombing all emphasise the difficulty of interpreting the past and achieving any certainty.

The early twenty-first century has demonstrated the power of language through the use of political slogans. These are short, easily absorbed and remembered phrases. Donald Trump in the United States seems to have won the presidency with the help of his slogan 'Make America great again', which every individual could take as a way to share in a social triumph. Any serious analysis of the phrase would indicate that such a position would lead to hostility from the rest of the world but slogans do not invite reflection. An equivalent slogan in the UK was seen in the parliamentary election of 2019 where Boris Johnson won a landslide victory with the use of a slogan demanding Britain's exit from the European Union: 'Get Brexit done'. No-one was invited to consider what this would do to the country. It was just an offer to clear up an irritating problem while respecting the votes cast in 2016 when just over half the country had voted to leave the European Union. The slogan that won that vote had been equally effective: 'Take back control'.

These examples show the powerful effect of a good slogan and also show how self-respect and self-confidence are bound up with social identity.

The West's involvement in the Iraq War of 2001 to 2011 demonstrated the effect of conviction. It arose from the ashes of the World Trade Center by talion law. The motivation was revenge. Politicians had to make this seem acceptable by using phrases like 'weapons of mass destruction'. The impact of such a phrase seems to be that there is so much horror involved that people will not wish to dwell on it or reflect on its likelihood. The effort to avoid the guilt for supporting aggression can lead to negative consequences. Many in the West were strongly opposed to the Iraq war of 2001 to 2011 and would not accept the powerful propaganda. Politicians like Robin Cook and Clare Short in the UK sacrificed their careers, resigning because they believed that the war was wrong. They of course had their own certainties, which convinced them that they could not honourably stay in post.

In order to assert the virtue of resigning, both these politicians had to achieve enough certainty to risk losing a successful career. Political certainties are often passionately held and can lead to family disputes and even separations. Referenda are particularly likely to lead to these sorts of divisions because they ask one simple, often highly simplified question. The demand is that all good citizens should align themselves with one side or the other in order to vote and having done so, there is a need for commitment. The process then enters the area where an individual might have to admit that he was wrong. Questions with more room for a grey area are less divisive and demand less sense of shame from the individual who might admit that his first choice no longer expresses the view that he holds.

Andrew Samuels (1993) explored the need for pluralism in the psyche with particular reference to politics; his ideas show the need for a change from valuing certainty without evidence. We can see by a short examination of the mass media in the twenty-first century that there are words like 'U-turn', which the media in general take to be a term of abuse. No politician is pleased to be met with headlines about a change of policy presented as a U-turn. In order to be elected, a politician is generally considered to need to convey confidence, and confidence is associated with certainty.

Political manifestos require promises to be made. Promises are a way of making a firm statement about the future. They can be phrased to allow a way out by means of provisos such as 'if conditions permit' or 'assuming the finances work out'. This is a sort of certainty that is not necessarily owned by the maker of the promise but is intended to be conveyed to the recipients of the message. By listening to the promises of a presidential candidate, the masses in the United States are carried forwards by the power of the group into a sort of certainty for which they may have no good reason at all but for which they may have every reason to hope. Candidates at each end of the political spectrum will offer a move towards a particular social paradise. It may be State ownership of the means of production, leading to a fair share for all citizens of the wealth that the community is capable of producing or it may be the freedom for each individual to pursue wealth and happiness in his or her own way. While it is very unlikely that any candidate could realise this sort of ambition, it is possible that he or she could contribute towards a trend in that direction. Voters will not see it in these vague and unsatisfactory terms and will rejoice in the certainty that they know what will happen if their candidate is elected.

This raises the predisposition of any of us to wish for the truth of a belief, which is an important element in the search for certainty. This is clearer in religion and politics than in most other spheres of human life. In both areas we can understand the strength of this wish in preventing the followers of any belief system from changing their minds. If someone gives up any aspect of the belief-system she risks that the rest of it may not be reliable. If the candidate fails to deliver one promise, she might lose your confidence in the rest of her integrity. In the same way, if you give up your belief in purgatory, you might lose the whole of life after death.

Since holding on to certainties has such an impact on all of us, it is important to consider also how this dead stop can be mitigated so that a change of mind might not only be acceptable but might also be seen to be desirable for a better quality of life. Andrew Samuels (1993) expressed the need for this change in *The Plural Psyche*. He set out to establish that the aim of what he called 'depth psychology' should be to achieve an attitude in which pluralism is possible. Pluralism is different from eclecticism but both terms relate to the theory by which one thinks or lives one's life. In terms of theory this is important for psychological therapists but it is important in terms of religion, politics and cultural ideology for each individual. Samuels laid out some of the problems facing anyone who does not believe that that there is one truth that contains all truths, which might be like the ring of power that binds all the others in *The Lord of the Rings* (Tolkien 1954). Samuels pointed out the emotional domain that we are considering:

> It is very hard to feel passionate about being tolerant ... to go in for what Walter Bagehot called 'animated toleration'.
>
> (Samuels 1993: 6)

A pluralist might be someone who comes to know less and less about more and more, never settling to any one belief or line of enquiry. Samuels was emphatic that he is speaking of the ability to see the edges of what one does not know. Of course, these edges are tricky places to be. Donald Rumsfeld, US Secretary of Defense (2001–2006), was the butt of much merriment when he spoke about the 'known unknowns' but this is in fact a valuable concept. There must be areas that we know we don't know and also areas where we do not know the edges of our knowledge. There are areas of an ice field where there is a risk of falling into a chasm, especially if we had no idea that chasms exist and had not tried to probe the solidity of the ground.

The language of religious certainties

What enables us to hold to a belief in the face of contradiction and maybe opposing evidence? One of the most important mechanisms in supporting internal conviction is the defense known as splitting. Melanie Klein's theory of internal objects brings with it the concept of an 'internal world' in which good objects (people usually) can be destroyed by bad objects just as they can in the outside world. An infant comes to believe that the only way to preserve good objects is to keep them separate from bad objects and this paves the way to an option of splitting as an emotional position to protect from any attack (Klein 1946).

In an external context like 9/11 attack, other emotions apart from rage and frustration must be protected. This splitting is greatly helped by identifying people or things to blame. This is clear and can happen on a public or private scale. There is also the complication of guilt, which can be unspecific and therefore uncertain but seeks certainty through self-blame.

Thinking goes along these lines: we, identifying with a majority in our society, treated Muslims badly and therefore we can understand their anger. At the extreme end of this is what we have come to know as radicalisation. This narrative argues that the West deserves atrocities because our governments have fought against and hurt Muslims in all sorts of contexts.

Because religion is another major source of these sorts of difficulty I have considered it separately in Chapter 4. Any psychological therapist is likely to encounter people who are suffering from the difference between their parents' religious position and their own. This can work in either direction. George Lakoff (2016) sees all morality as using the metaphors of the family in which the State or the church become the strict father or the nurturing parent. He examines conservative and liberal points of view that are held with passionate conviction and considers that they are based on different family structures. Sometimes the parents are liberal atheists or agnostics and they cannot understand children who in the time-honoured way rebel by finding a religious belief system or sect to replace the perceived vagueness of the parents. On the other hand, we encounter the children of parents with strict religious views, as in such sects as Plymouth Brethren or Jehovah's Witnesses. Most sects have ways of excluding those who cease to go along with their beliefs. Christian Scientists, for example, use the process of *shunning* in which those who cease to believe in the tenets of the sect are excluded from all association with its members. The people who are treated this way or who fear it are likely to continue to conform to the required practices of the institution even if they cannot truly subscribe to the beliefs. We cannot know how much such practices might compel a form of belief in the end. This process might describe what we think of as *brainwashing*.

If we consider this process we will return to the analysis of guilt and the way in which it works at every level of fundamentalism. Josiah was a young man of 19, who came to see me for therapy. His parents were Jehovah's Witnesses and he described a childhood that had been in many ways a good experience even though his parents had been strict by any standards. He felt that they had been clear about the rules and were fair to him. His younger sister however was treated differently from him. It was because of what he perceived as unfair treatment of girls that he began to question the whole basis of the faith that he was being required to accept. He found it very difficult to come to a therapist because he knew that this might become a great betrayal of the values he had been taught. He was very timid and cautious at first and would say nothing against his family or his background and yet his mere presence in my consulting room showed us both that he was not at peace with his past.

As time went by, he was able to talk a little. Even though I was acutely aware of the risk that he was running to his world view in letting me know about his doubts, I waited for him to be able to express what those doubts were. In a later chapter I will develop a view of the sorts of problems that fundamentalism of this sort brings to the people involved and from that discussion will open questions about how we can help.

In another case, a Roman Catholic nun came to see a psychotherapist because she was thinking she might leave her order. This had caused her great distress. Her spiritual adviser had allowed her to seek a lay therapist who would not necessarily share her religious faith. She was very concerned to discover whether the therapist was a Christian or not. She asked in the first meeting and the therapist pointed out that she might well have anxieties about whether the therapist would be an atheist and want her to leave or a devoted Christian who would encourage her to stay. In fact, she did not need either of these responses but someone who could listen to her own position and help her to understand it and her reasons. This was a difficult task for the therapist, who was aware that anything she said could be misunderstood and applied to one side or the other.

The language of the body

We need to consider all aspects of human life and not just the social areas of religion and politics. Health for example is an area where there is a great need for some of the confidence that arises from certainty. Chapters on depression and the autistic spectrum look at various aspects of health. A surgeon conducting an operation on BBC television in January 2018 set out to excise a very large sarcoma from a woman's body. He knew with certainty that the sarcoma would kill her if he did not remove it. It had already enveloped one of her kidneys and was continuing to grow. He also had his certainties about how the removal must be conducted. He had to reconnect blood vessels that he would disrupt. He had to ensure that no part of the tumour was left behind to seed itself. But as he opened the abdominal cavity, he did not recognise the way in which the organs had been displaced by the tumour. He could not tell which blood vessels were which and therefore did not know which was feeding the vital kidney that was functioning. In this situation he had to rely on his certainties and from them he had to be willing to discover what needed to be done.

Unwarranted certainty in the field of health can do a great deal of harm. Many aspects of health affect the individual. Diet is one of the most obvious areas where we are told at intervals what will be best to eat and drink. We are troubled by the inevitability of death and the understanding that living leads in that one direction. The hope of slowing the process down makes many of us eager to read about research findings that seem to tell us what will lead to cancer, stroke, heart disease — all the demons that dog our footsteps. We eat or do not eat accordingly and very few people have the leisure or the knowledge to assess the research in any useful or rational way from primary texts. When we do examine research, we often find much less than certainty. For example, the genetic component of obesity has attracted a great deal of attention as one way of addressing one of the greatest health problems of the Western world. If it could be established with certainty that a predisposition to overeat is linked to the presence of a particular gene, there would be great excitement as it would lead to all sorts of new commercial opportunities for treatment and also the people suffering from obesity would be able to be freed from the guilt that their condition arises from self-indulgence and lack of will power. So far, the genetic links have caused some misapprehension. Leptin is a hormone that was thought to control appetite and the sense of fullness. In fact, its action is much more complex and what is needed in considering its effect for the ordinary person trying to lose weight is an open lack of certainty. There is a combination of psychological motivation to lose weight and hormonally induced predispositions. There is no easy solution to this problem but it illustrates how much desire there might be for a solution.

Certainty in fiction

George Orwell's satires focus on the power of language. In *1984* (Orwell 1949) the government plans to exercise control by various means but one important one is to make everyone speak Newspeak, a language that will not allow for rebellious thoughts. Propaganda is run by the Ministry for Truth. *Animal Farm* (Orwell 1945) also makes clear the value of language in creating new certainties and controlling the population in this way. Most people will remember the pigs' slogan, 'All animals are equal', which later was changed to 'All animals are equal but some are more equal than others'. A different view of the desire for certainty can be found in the interest in art and literature. Detective fiction shows a movement through the setting of a puzzle, the exploration of various possible solutions and at the very end a certainty is usually achieved in the resolution. If the writer has left any of the strands unresolved, most readers will feel cheated or even angry. A more complex and interesting story will almost certainly leave some questions unanswered. Mohsin Hamid (2007) in *The Reluctant Fundamentalist* used the technique of ambiguity and uncertainty to hold and also to frustrate his readers. On the other hand, his novel met with acclaim and has met with comments such as 'makes you think' from the *Daily Telegraph* (2007).

We can therefore look at the use of certainty and uncertainty in the arts as a way of engaging the participant and making her involved in a process rather than offering her something that is already complete. This echoes the process that needs to take in place in a therapeutic setting where old convictions can be seen to be harmful and need to be reconsidered.

Certainty and mental health

Not surprisingly a person's need for certainty and the way in which it affects their experience enters into any recognisable mental condition or illness. We can establish the need and wish for certainty in all areas of human life. What is more difficult is to develop ideas about how we can use this wish to make human relationships more tolerant and constructive. Depression is a form of imprisonment in which the gaoler is also the prisoner and will allow no escape. The certainty of beliefs about the self forms the walls and bars of the prison. Autism and Asperger's syndrome are also based on the need for certainty. The obsessive person is constantly searching for safety by checking his uncertainties – 'Did I switch the gas taps off?' To some extent we all need the certainties that are sought. The taps should be turned off but the uncertainty becomes a sickness that can never be cured unless the reason for it is understood and help is given.

One of the most difficult questions to answer is about the origin and development of the wish for certainty in each individual. This will be addressed in each of the following chapters. Contemporary fundamentalism is often associated in popular culture with violence and sadism. Jessica Benjamin (2002), writing soon after the attack on the Twin Towers, considered the importance of guilt and self-righteousness and the way in which the two interact. This is an important element of the fundamentalism that therapists might see in the consulting room. Every therapist herself might experience guilt at some point for what has been done badly or not done at all and what we do with this guilt is vital both for our own health and for the sake of the patient. It also illustrates the process that might develop in anyone. Benjamin usefully confronts the tendency to split as the response to fundamentalist attacks. Because we are all dealing with fear of weakness and ultimately death, we are all subject to the wish to evacuate feelings of weakness and fear and to experience instead self-righteousness and moralism. She emphasises how much danger lies in the inevitable consulting room split: 'I sit in my therapist's chair while you are over there as the patient'. Here is the point at which the therapist must face her own fears and her own wish to eliminate guilt.

Perhaps the small child learns from the earliest experiences to see himself on the side of virtue: 'It wasn't me. It was my sister'. The power of the guilt and anxiety experienced in each of us is such that we may develop rigid defensive structures in the mind to protect us from the inner attacks of conscience or the superego. Ruth Stein (2006) uses the metaphor of a carapace to describe the sense of a hard, rigid shell surrounding the terrified, persecuted ego that has survived from childhood. If we take her central image of the vertical structuring of the psyche, we have an all-powerful god, superior to a man who is superior to unbelievers and to all women. The believer knows that his god/father is right. His superego wishes to make him persecute others, not himself, as punishment for his forbidden wishes. We also have the myth of the father whose god or superego tells him to sacrifice his son. This of course took on terrible reality for those who lived through the two great wars of the twentieth century in which older men sent the younger men to their deaths. If this image represents a psychic reality, there would be no surprise if the son were filled with hatred against the all-powerful established father, as well as with paradoxical love for him. This sounds confusing even though the fundamentalist is trying desperately to avoid any kind of confusion. Defences against this dilemma are the probable result and will form the subject of this book.

References

BBC Monitoring. (2001) 'In full: Al-Qaeda statement' 10 Oct 2001.

Benjamin, J. (2002) 'Terror and guilt' *Psychoanalytic Dialogues* 12(3): 473–484.

Coleman, W. (2019) 'The analytic superego' in Hardin, C. (Ed.), *Dissecting the Superego* (pp. 179–186). London: Routledge.

Goodstein, L. (2001) 'Falwell: blame abortionists, feminists and gays' *New York Times*, 19 Sep 2001.

Hamid, M. (2007) *The Reluctant Fundamentalist*. London: Penguin Books.

Hamilton, C. (1991) *The Hitler Diaries*. Lexington: The University Press of Kentucky.

Harding, C. (Ed.) (2019) *Dissecting the Superego*. London: Routledge.

Lakoff, G. (2016) *Moral Politics*. Chicago: University of Chicago Press.

MacArthur, B. (1991) 'Up in smoke' *The Sunday Times*, London. 9 Jun 1991, p. 1, section 3.

Mahler, J. (2015) 'What do we really know about Osama bin Laden's death?' *New York Times*, 15 Oct 2015.

Orwell, G. (1945) *Animal Farm*. London: Secker and Warburg.

Orwell, G. (1949) *Nineteen Eighty Four: A Novel*. London: Secker and Warburg.

Pinker, S. (1994) *The Language Instinct*. New York: William Morrow and Company.

Rosling, H. (2018) *Factfulness*. London: Hodder and Stoughton.

Samuels, A. (1993) *The Political Psyche*. London: Routledge.

Stein, R. (2006) 'Fundamentalism, father and son and vertical desire' *Psychoanalytic Review* 93(2): 201–229.

Summers, F. (2006) 'Fundamentalism, psychoanalysis, and psychoanalytic theories' *Psychoanalytic Review* 93(2): 329–352.

Tolkien, J.R. (1954) *Lord of the Rings*. London: George Allen & Unwin.

Whorf, B.L. (1956) 'Science and linguistics' in Carroll, J.B. (Ed.), *Language, Thought, and Reality: Selected Writings of Benjamin Lee Whorf* (pp. 151–203). Cambridge, MA: MIT Press.

Yeats, W.B. (1976) *Collected Poems of W. B. Yeats*. Richmond: Setanta Books.

Chapter 2

Certainty in everyday life

Doubt thou the stars are fire
Doubt that the sun doth move
Doubt truth to be a liar
But never doubt I love
      William Shakespeare,
        Hamlet, 1609

Assurances like Hamlet's ditty to Ophelia need to be examined. This chapter is about the part played by conviction in families and in close relationships and considers how such convictions are formed and how they can cause damage. If they are harmful, or ill-founded they need to change and the question is whether and how this can happen.

Shakespeare's *Hamlet* is a play about the doubt and uncertainty in Hamlet's life. Most people know the question that he raises about whether life is worth living – the soliloquy begins 'To be or not to be?' (Act III, scene i, 34–98). This is only one aspect of his urgent wish to be certain. Did the ghost of his father really appear? Was the ghost of his father right in telling him that his uncle was a murderer? Would he be justified in killing his uncle in revenge and if so when? Whom at court could he trust? Hamlet wrote the ditty to Ophelia that opens this chapter and, although the play is focused on his mother's sexuality, we can see that Hamlet is tormented by the impact that it has on his own love. In obedience to her father, she gives him back his letters and poems. He says to her: 'I did love you once'. Her response is: 'Indeed, my lord, you made me believe so'. He turns on her at once for her trusting certainty: 'You should not have believed me'. Hamlet is so hurt by his mother's behaviour that he hurts Ophelia in turn: 'I loved you not'.

Ophelia is driven to suicide when Hamlet deserts her. We can see this as one point where Hamlet has achieved a disastrous certainty. Women are deceivers and not to be trusted. The audience knows that, in his mind, he is speaking to his mother at this point but there is no doubt in his mind when he shouts at Ophelia to get herself off to a nunnery.

Doubt can lead to unwarranted certainty

Hamlet is tormented by the question of whether he can believe in the ghost or believe the ghost enough to kill his uncle. Luckily most of us have less dramatic questions but everyone has the problem of sifting through all the information that we get every day to find what is true. Some questions like the reality of climate change can be resolved by referring to various independent observations and the causes can potentially be established by use of the scientific method. Most of the important questions of everyday life have much less reliable sources of information to help in decision making. How do you know when someone is lying? What do you consider to be adequate evidence one way or the other. Technology has made the task more difficult as images can be changed to an extent that is totally misleading. Photographs can be altered so that a new face is added to a figure and everyone believes that they have seen an action take place. They may be deceived. We enjoy that facility when used in special effects in films but it makes some people resort to passionate but unfounded conviction and others to perpetual doubt.

Shakespeare shows us in Hamlet's tragic story some of the ways in which doubt can be resolved in disastrous certainty. Ophelia's disillusionment is disastrous. She drowns herself. Both doubt and certainty affect us in more ordinary relationships. Therapists see the working of uncertainty in myriad ways but one of the most common is in jealousy. As soon as we are born, we need to feel sure that the mother who gave birth to us will feed, clean, warm us and above all will not leave the helpless infant alone. For the rest of life there is a question: can I survive without another person? This leads people to seek therapy because they have been unable to form a stable relationship with another. For some the matter becomes a social question: can I enjoy my life alone? It leads others to seek therapy out of fear that they will spoil a good relationship through jealousy and fear.

The role of anxiety

Parents will come to a therapist out of anxiety about their children. Some of the chaos in *Hamlet* is caused by Claudius wanting to make himself safe from accusations of murder but some of it is caused by Gertrude who has some of the qualities of an anxious mother. She knows that the trouble with Hamlet is not just that Ophelia has obeyed her father's instructions and returned his letters and rejected his poems. Of course, there is the terrible scene in which he tells Gertrude what he thinks of her for marrying within a month of her husband's death but before that she is very disturbed about Hamlet's wanting to leave home again to study and she begs him to stay. She allows Polonius to spy on him in the hope that they can cure his apparent madness. At the end she is again concerned about him and wipes his brow in the final fatal duel and it is drinking to his success that poisons her and kills her. As she is dying, she is clear and certain and will allow no more deception: 'No, no the drink. Oh, my dear Hamlet, the drink, the drink, I am poisoned' (*Hamlet*, Act V, scene i, 303–304).

Truth and certainty

This brief look at *Hamlet* brings us inevitably to the importance of truth. If I believe that it is true that the Earth is warming because of man's actions then I must by definition be certain of it. Truth requires certainty. If I say that X is true it is a tautology to say that I am certain of it. The next two chapters will focus particularly on politics and religion but they are both spheres which are inextricably involved in the way in which we relate to each other through our convictions.

Since the post-modernist concept of truth is to view it in many versions and not as though it were reducible to one absolute, the developing change in the twenty-first century seems to be to expect the individual to partici-pate in making her own truth. We have seen the rise of populism in politics where people are encouraged to say, 'This is my opinion' and to ignore evi-dence. We now also see the importance attached to participatory television by voting in contest programmes and writing comments both there and on social media. Games now often involve the creation of avatars that may carry some of an individual's sense of self into a struggle against the powers of darkness. National leaders of the twenty-first century seem to take the view that truth is what each person wants it to be and outright lying is no longer a matter for shame. No doubt this too will pass but it leads to a very high level of personal conviction combined with a low level of general socially held certainty.

Children develop a view of the world that may involve religious or moral certainties but will involve beliefs about authorities, such as those who care for them. Theories of child development consider the ways in which paren-tal voices as well as the social norms of the environment enter the child's superego. The child psychiatrist Donald Winnicott (1963) emphasised the importance of the nurturing figure, usually the mother, in developing the child's way of relating to others. He named two aspects of the child's view of his mother. One is the mother to whom the child addresses his funda-mental needs and desires, which we recognise in all the rage of an angry baby as devouring and destructive. The other is the survivor mother to whom he could make reparation for his rage. Although Winnicott does not talk in terms of certainty or conviction, his theory implies that the child comes to believe in his own capacity to make reparation. This conviction is the foundation of caring for someone else and leads to empathy and a way of moving beyond harmful guilt.

The role of empathy

Empathy is a cure for certainty. No-one can know for certain what another feels or thinks but the effort to try to understand is part of what makes relationships work. In favourable circumstances, the mother by continuing to be alive and available is both the mother who receives all the full impact of the baby's demands, and also the mother who can be loved as a person and to whom reparation for crimes real or imagined, can be made. In this way, the anxiety about the demands becomes tolerable to the baby, who can then experience guilt, or can hold it until an opportunity to make reparation for it. To this guilt that is held but not felt as such, we give the name 'concern'. In the initial stages of development, without a reliable mother-figure to receive the reparation the guilt becomes intolerable, and anger and hate take the place of love and empathy. Failure of reparation leads to a losing of the capacity for concern, and to its replacement by primitive forms of guilt and anxiety (Winnicott 1963: 73–81). The development of empathy is a crucial process for a child who will not be able to make positive relationships with others if she cannot accept that there are minds other than her own. The child who is frightened, threatened or neglected may retreat into certainties of her own as a protection from the vagaries of the unpredictable Other. Some children stay in this stage and will be exhibiting the difficulties that will make future relationships very difficult for them.

The role of parents in forming the language of certainty

Parental style will have an impact on the child's belief system. George Lakoff (2016) discussed the effect of parental style on the convictions of the older child. He considers the impact of the strict disciplinarian parent, usually designated as the father, as opposed to the lax or neglectful parent:

> [Y]ou simply tell the child what to do and punish him if he doesn't do it. What is going wrong is that you are not nurturing the child, not teaching empathy so that he will know how to behave responsibly in new situations where empathy, not strict rules is the guide to appropriate behaviour. If you give and enforce orders you are not contributing to trust and responsible independence.
>
> (2016: 312)

Strict fathers may impose any kind of rules but are most likely to try to impose their own beliefs in the form of religion or culture. This statement is misleading in that, although it is true, it leaves out the soft power of the mother figure. She is a powerful guardian of culture and will pass on her own certainties to her children even if she sometimes does it with the emotional threats of being profoundly hurt by deviations.

One of the examples argued by Lakoff (2016) is the matter of abortion and women's choice versus the right to life lobby. He argues that each side is locked into its position by the choice of words that solidify into certainties. He considers the terminology: there is a cluster of cells that becomes an embryo which then becomes a foetus, a recognisable precursor of a human shape at eight to 12 weeks. These are medical terms and can suggest that pregnancy is a medical matter so that problems have a medical solution. If, however, you choose to call the embryo or foetus a 'baby' there is a very different emotional connotation. A baby, Lakoff argues, is a foetus after it is born and is capable of independent life. By the different use of these terms, a proponent of one view or the other shows total conviction of the morality of their own position and the wickedness or unreason of the other side. The fact that we talk of a 'choice' of words implies that there is another certainty beneath. Lakoff would argue that we are still in the territory of the strict father and that this is a model that provides us with certainties from which we choose our positions throughout life (2016: 208).

The novel *A Song for Issy Bradley*, written by Carys Bray (2014), shows a father imposing his Mormon beliefs on his family. Bray shows us her view of the impact of the Mormon church on a family when the much-loved youngest child, four-year-old Issy, dies of meningitis. On the morning when her illness begins, Jacob, who is seven, wakes up for his birthday with enormous anticipation. His father is a Mormon bishop and when one of his flock, Sister Anderson, asks for his help he goes immediately and will not be able to eat breakfast with his family. He is already missing the birthday party: 'Of course, I'll come to a missionary meeting on Sunday. I'll miss Jacob's party but I'm sure he'll understand' (2014: 18).

Ian does not know that his little daughter is already dying from meningitis. The whole novel is about the impact of the father's certainty in his religious beliefs and way in which they affect and spoil his children's lives and stunt his wife. What gives the novel its power and impact is the complexity that it reveals. Bishop Bradley is not a simple bully. He loves his wife and his children and his faith gives him no difficulty. What is problematic for him is his own narcissistic need to be seen to be doing the work of the Mormon church. This aspect of what Andre Green refers to as 'moral narcissism' (1981) is so entangled with his belief in his religion that he cannot think about it. Although he is able to keep to his beliefs as far as we know, he suffers more and more from acid reflux. This becomes a symbol of the way in which he is attacked from within as well as from the behaviour of others in particular his wife. Acid is the image of the bitterness he experiences. He tries to maintain his conviction by saying to himself and his family that the sacrifices that he imposes on himself and on them are nothing compared with the hardships of the pioneers who crossed the United States to Salt Lake City, and in any case the reward will be great.

The novel begins with situations that will be familiar to many people. Ian's conviction that he should put others first leads him to disappoint his little boy. Helping Sister Anderson will take him away from the family breakfast but because the ideal of helping others is important to him, he agrees to do it and deprive his son. In doing this he is being a Strict Father in Lakoff's terms. He expects his son to accept his valuation of the situation and gives him no choice. In doing so, a man like this would no doubt think that he was teaching his son to take the values of community service as weighing much more than pleasing his family.

Certainty in the family drama

The more general point that Carys Bray makes in her novel is that conviction of the importance of religious values can take precedence over everything else in the minds of proponents. Ian requires his family to accept his values, which must not be questioned. He has already demanded that his wife, Claire, should accept the whole teaching of the Mormon church, which involves more in the daily customs than most other churches. For example, it is forbidden to drink tea or coffee, never mind alcohol. Alma suffers when his friend's father, Steve, offers to get Ian a cup of tea at the football match but Ian says, 'I don't drink tea' and Al worries that this will make a 'missionary opportunity' if Steve asks why not. This is a very small interchange but it demonstrates the way in which the children suffer from being different in relationships with friends who are not part of the fundamentalism concerned. Claire also suffers from the way in which religion becomes culture and dominates the whole of her life. She accepts much of the teaching that was required in order to marry Ian but we are shown a small thought rebellion when, missing her mother who is dead, she wishes that she could sit with a comforting mug of tea the way she would have done with her mother:

> It's been more than seventeen years since she's had tea, just one cup would be enough to disqualify her from the Temple.
>
> (2014: 290)

Claire lost her mother and her little girl and she seems lost herself. The book leaves the reader with questions because it is framed by Claire going to the beach at the beginning and at the end. She had a dream that says that God speaks to her on the beach and says that he loves her. At the end of the book we see her at the beach but we are left unsure whether she will drown or save herself before the tide overwhelms her. She has longed for her lost daughter but at the very end we are told that she 'turns towards home'. The loss of one daughter must be mitigated by the needs of the daughter she still has as well as her husband and her two sons. The book is enclosed by the two images of Claire going to the beach as a symbol of transition, but Carys Bray leaves us uncertain about whether she can get back to the shore. The impact of the novel is to reveal the profound uncertainty of human life and death and the ways in which we make our sadness worse by taking up rigid positions.

The approach of the incoming tide is, of course, a metaphor for the struggle that we have seen in Claire's mind. The tide threatens to overwhelm her and the sand beneath her feet is not secure. She took on the faith of her husband when she married Ian but it has not been easy for her. In a flashback we are told about how a Mormon wedding progresses. Claire was to take off all her clothes and be anointed by older women. She was then allowed to put on her wedding dress but, as it was considered too revealing of her arms and neck, she was draped with other material to make her more modest. The ceremony itself, which took place in the Temple, had different promises for men and for women. She would 'give' herself to Ian. He would 'receive' her. This disparity bothered her for some time but after a while she had reconciled herself to it until her daughter, Issy, died when the whole question of her own inadequacy to meet the standards of the church became overwhelming.

Claire retreats to Issy's bed and Ian tells everyone that she is ill. One of the women in the church, Sister Valentine comes to see her one day to point out something that she is sure will be a great relief to Claire: she will marry Ian and look after him when Claire dies. This goes along with the comment by Ian's mother that polygamy is not practised currently but is still the ideal. The whole novel puts emphasis on the powerlessness of women and the consequent importance of marriage. They are to enjoy procreation in order to increase the number of members of the Mormon church. This is to be a woman's only, or at least main, purpose in life. This takes some accepting and we see the effect on the older daughter Zipporah as well.

The woman in charge of youth education sets up a wedding practice for the girls of Zipporah's age in which they are each to wear their mother's wedding dress and parade down an imaginary aisle. Afterwards they fill in a form with a description of the imaginary bridegroom and imaginary names for their imaginary future children. All this can be read as indoctrination of the girls of this society with the acceptance of their destiny. The other side of the insistence on this ethic of marriage is the utter condemnation of any kind of sexual interest or desire outside of marriage. This is not of course restricted to Mormons and is a part of all sorts of fundamentalism, most of which insist on the control and restriction of women and female sexuality. This has, of course set up reciprocal fundamentalism among feminists who can be equally resistant to reason or humanity.

Sexuality produces another kind of certainty

Marriage among Mormons will be arranged by the parents and all uncertainty created by choice will be eliminated. Zipporah goes through the normal teenage response to her hormones and feels fascinated by a boy, Adam. At one point he kisses her and she discovers that she likes it. She has to confess what is regarded as a great sin to the President of the District. Later she tries to talk to her mother but Claire misunderstands and is so wrapped up in her own sense of inadequacy and her fear that her lack of faith caused the death of her four-year-old that she cannot pay attention to the living daughter who needs her.

Each member of the family is affected in different ways by the demands of belief and the community. Jacob whose seventh birthday opens the novel is profoundly affected by the death of his little sister. He takes on the stories of miracles and resurrection and sets out to resurrect his sister. He has been taught that, if he can pray very hard, the Heavenly Father will listen. These beliefs were taught as certainties but he still knows that he has to work hard to bring about a miracle. He sets out to practise by resurrecting his goldfish, Fred.

> It was OK to kill Fred because firstly if he prayed very hard and Fred was resurrected, it would prove that Issy could come back too.
>
> (2014: 248)

Jacob is not sure that he can get Heavenly Father to bring his sister back to life but he carries out the experiment with Fred the goldfish and because Ian, his father, sees the dead fish and replaces it with a live one so that the children will not be upset by another death, Jacob is able to believe that his prayers have been answered. He is disillusioned by his Father who tells him that he had replaced the dead goldfish. Later Ian tells Jacob that praying is not like making a Christmas list. You can't just ask for anything you want. Ian reacts strongly to his two sons both showing questioning in different ways. He tells Jacob for example that Father Christmas is not real. Jacob's response is logical: 'If Father Christmas is not real, is Jesus real?' Alma, the older son, is also questioning and Jacob wants his beliefs reaffirmed. At this point Ian is reaffirming the certainty on which his whole life is built and is 'so intent on being right that he forgets to be kind' (2014: 360). Zipporah sees how much he is hurting Jacob at this point and tries to comfort her little brother, wanting to take the place of the mother who is not able to help at all. These children illustrate the ways in which children are given parental beliefs but have to arrive at convictions that they can hold for themselves.

Certainty affects the body

Therapists will encounter people who have been affected by a diagnosis of health problems, some of them telling of a terminal illness either for themselves or for someone close. How much does the mind-set of the person receiving the diagnosis affect the ability to manage the impact of potential suffering and death on their lives? Some people are strongly convinced that the emotional reaction of the person to the illness will make a difference to how the body deals with it.

Mavis, a young woman in her 30s working in marketing, came to see a therapist when she had a diagnosis of breast cancer. She was told that it was metastatic and, as she was suffering from painful headaches, she had great anxiety that she had a brain tumour. She was gathering her courage to go to her consultant and see what he would say. She told her therapist that she had spoken to people at work about her fears and they said that she must have a positive attitude to 'fight' the cancer. She also saw the publicity of charities which talked of 'battling cancer' implying that those who were able to have a positive attitude would be able to survive.

Mavis went to see her consultant and it turned out that she had a small brain tumour. She was shocked and appalled because she believed that it was her own fault. She had not been sufficiently certain that she could win the fight. The therapist was also distressed but saw her task as helping Mavis to accept the physical nature of the tumour and the appropriateness of her own feelings of distress about it. Guilt needed to be accepted and consigned to the various places where it belonged so that reparation could be made. If the cancer turned out to be terminal the therapist wished to help her to a good death but was anxious not to arrive at premature convictions about what would happen.

Conviction in relationships

Most of the people who work with those who are suffering mentally will have come across a few people who are bothered with a crisis of religious faith and that will be looked at in more depth in Chapter 4. What is even more common is the human distress caused by our convictions in relation to each other. This occurs in surprising places as well as in the more predictable matters of money and occupation. In *A Song for Issy Bradley*, the religious conviction began with the Father. Obeying the Mormon faith, he tries to be the wise *pater familias*, passing on the faith that he derived from his own, evidently righteous parents. They are so convinced of the importance of their missionary work in England that they will not fly home for the funeral of their granddaughter. Ian passed this faith on as best he could to his wife and children. There is just as much difficulty in the conviction that must be passed on in other connections.

Helen is a busy lawyer who came to me for therapy. She had a successful career behind her. She was almost ready for retirement and was trying to face what that would mean for her. She has had to be strong and determined to achieve as much as she has in her career but she could not see how she would be able to use those qualities in her retirement. Her daughter had just had a baby and she was delighted to have a granddaughter although she was worried that she herself was, as she put it 'about to be scrapped'. She was afraid that her daughter would assume that she was completely free as she was retired and she resented her daughter's assumption that she could expect unlimited availability as a grandparental baby sitter.

In the meantime, Helen developed a role for herself as protector of the little girl. She saw the baby's father coming in from work and giving her a little shake while tickling her. The baby seemed surprised but not, as Helen always pointed out, frightened. She thought that this treatment was too rough and she became very concerned that she should say something to her daughter. We could both see that she was putting herself into the role of the lawyer who could help and protect her clients and thus the fears had served a useful purpose for Helen. They also caused her distress and she was very anxious that if she spoke to her daughter it might damage that relationship and also the daughter's relationship with her husband. She said to me many times, 'I just think it is wrong that he is so rough with the baby when she is so tiny and defenceless'.

After some time, she began to see for herself that she was making a great deal of effort to maintain this narrative against her own repeated interjections 'I'm sure that Marion is really fine and, also, I can see that George really loves her and wouldn't harm her. I just am not happy with this habit of his'. I asked whether she was worried that this was something near shaken baby syndrome. This made her angry. 'No, of course not. I can see perfectly well that it's nothing like that'. There was a pause. 'I've been talking as though it was though, haven't I?' Another pause. 'Why on earth am I doing that?'

Helen was a very perceptive patient and she began to investigate her own need for this particular conviction and began to see some of her wish to be the mother of the baby, not just the grandmother. From that position she began to see the benefits of her position and started to feel some of the traditional benefits of her role. 'It's true that there are advantages to being able to go home for a good night's sleep'.

Helen stepped back from the possibility of a rift with her son in law just at a time when she was most needed to be patient and understanding and provide a framework of stability for the new parents.

Adult relationships

Helen's experience raises the importance of an open mind in relationships. Dogmatic parents have caused much misery both to young children and to the adults who grow from them as Carys Bray has shown in her novel (2014). In clinical practice another area of experience is in the making and holding of emotional connections between adults.

Andrew is young man of 26 who has had no long-term relationships although he has met Florence, a woman of 18 on a beach. They got on very well but she wanted to go on round the world as it was a gap year for her but he had to get back to his work as a junior doctor. They met on and off when she returned but she was very happy to stay independent and to take up her position with an engineering firm in a different city. Although he could never quite decide that she was not for him, Andrew suffered from a wish to make something work with her but was not able to drop his own training in order to be with her. He had some convictions that he had derived from his own divorced parents. One was that he could not put enough trust into the relationship to make plans for the future such as exploring the possibilities of hospitals in the area where she was working. He backed himself into a corner believing that he could not bear to live with her in case she left him but nor could he live without her.

The first task of the therapy with Andrew was to disentangle his own feelings from what he had seen in his parents so that he was able to think about Florence more as she was and less as she seemed through the filter of his mother's suffering and escape. This phase of the therapy lasted for six months or so and then he began to accuse the therapist of not helping him to make up his mind. Being angry left him unhappy and confused but it gave the therapist an opportunity to help him to see that he was angry with Florence for not making it easier for him and that he dared not express any of this for fear of becoming like his own violent father.

This was a difficult and very uncomfortable phase for the therapist who began to feel that he was not doing a good enough job in helping Andrew. On reflection he could see that this counter transference reaction would have some reality in it but might also help him to understand Andrew's difficulty in feeling that he could be good enough for Florence. This was a fear that he had been hiding from himself but needed to look at and assess. He got as far as thinking about whether Florence would accept the limitation on her freedom of having him living with her or even nearby. This had become a fixed idea in his mind and he discovered that he had been making up other reasons for not risking it.

Work-based uncertainty

Andrew shows us that uncertainty and self-doubt attract certainty and conviction to cover them over so that the subject does not have to recognise his own problems. Every clinician will encounter certainty as a defence to hide doubt. I will return to this theme in later chapters. One of the major areas of distress for most patients in early to late adulthood is over work of all sorts, paid and unpaid, in the home and outside. Areas of uncertainty need to be tracked down both in the patient and in the people he is finding difficult.

Jean came to see a therapist because she had been signed off sick from work. She said that the reason for this was the stress that she had suffered from a bullying boss. There had apparently been a difficulty because she had listed a qualification on her application form that was not strictly true. She listed a qualification which she was hoping to get in the summer and in fact did get, but the application was made in April. The Head of Department had asked her about how long she had been qualified and without thinking she gave the true answer. This led to a long process with HR and with interviews in which she tried to feel angry and badly treated while knowing that she had indeed committed an offence She said that she was 'almost ready to admit it' but that 'she [her manager] didn't give me a chance to explain'. The therapist was having some difficulty in empathising with this position. The manager had been told a lie and her actions arose from that certainty. Jean thought that she was being held at the point of this certainty in a way that was tyrannical. The difficulty in empathising with Jean is that she had clearly thought that the lie would help her to get the job. Her sense of entitlement enabled her to see it as unimportant and so close to the truth that she should not be held to account for it.

Rather than accepting her own ambivalence about the justice of Jean's position, the therapist arrived at supervision filled with her own certainty. She wanted to 'be on the side of the patient' and was certain that the manager had bullied her and that Jean needed the therapist to believe in the reality of the bullying. The supervisor had to consider the certainty to which she was exposed and noted that her own response to this was a retreat into a certainty of her own. She wanted to say that bullying is a subjective experience and can indicate someone with a victim mentality. She noted this and was able to introduce the idea as a question related to the way the therapist was talking about the client rather than as any form of criticism of the therapist's position. One question to ask might be 'Do you think that the client is presenting this to you with such conviction because there is a little whisper of uncertainty: a fear that someone else might see it differently?'

The task with harmful certainty in the patient is often to probe the underlying doubt, which is seeking reassurance through enforcing beliefs that must not be challenged.

The basis for certainty

Perhaps it is not surprising that each of us might seek to find some certainties to which we can anchor ourselves. What might once have constituted certainty – 'I read it in the paper' or 'I heard it on the radio' – have long since been shown to be questionable. Understanding something of what can be done by technology brings simple perception through the senses into question. Technology itself brings us doubts where once there was certainty. The more we know about neuroscience the more we understand that our own perceptions can be as difficult to interpret as the technology itself can be to a non-specialist.

In 2015, there was a brief but very widespread controversy on social media such as Facebook, Twitter and Tumblr over a picture of a dress to be worn at a wedding by a bride's mother. 60% of viewers saw the dress as coloured black and blue. However, the dress appeared white and gold to about 30%, with some people indecisive. The scientific explanation is complicated and uncertain, including variables such as the context and the time of day and the different ways in which we compensate for light conditions. But the example illustrates how deceived we can be by our senses. A similar example in 2018 was provided by an audio recording of the word 'Laurel', which was perceived as such by 53% of people surveyed but was heard as the name 'Yanny' by the rest. The outcome depends on the way the listener perceives high and low frequencies.

Both the picture of the dress and Laurel/Yanny are stimuli that are able to trigger two distinct sensory experiences Because the result is in a boundary area between the two, our consciousness doesn't like the ambiguity, and so when confronted with these sorts of stimuli our brains tend to generate an unambiguous perception: 'the dress is definitely white and gold' or 'I definitely heard Yanny'. We are, as usual, hard-wired to arrive at some sort of certainty and even those who were able to see both sets of colours alternately or hear both names, usually settled to one or the other. We have to trust our senses enough to walk down steps or avoid obstacles. We have to believe that we hear voices from the outside. If they are only in the head, we have to be able to distinguish them clearly from external reality. Otherwise we suffer the distress and fear of schizophrenia.

Although we might be aware of these occasional illustrations of doubt over our perceptions, we like to think that we can believe them and yet, such is the skill of computer science; almost anything can be made to appear as reality. As a result, the Courts might no longer take digital evidence as admissible: all the body cameras and CCTV that we now think protect us may gradually become useless as the images are too easy to fake:

> 'Deepfake' software can use machine learning to make convincing simulations of real people saying and doing things that they may never have said or done. A predictably swift and gross application has been to superimpose the faces of Hollywood actors on to the bodies of pornographic film actors.
>
> (Scott 2018)

What constitutes acceptable evidence?

Laurence Scott (2018), writing in *The Guardian*, points out that the New York State Assembly is proposing to make a State law that 'the use of a digital replica of an individual shall constitute a violation if done without the consent of that individual'. In this way an era in which the existence of a photograph or recording could be taken as indubitable evidence of truth is closing in a smother of fake news and alternative facts.

The clearest sense in which this relates to the therapeutic process has been in the false memories of abuse. The difficulty of reaching a true and fair verdict over what, by definition has usually happened in private between only the two people concerned is exacerbated by the doubt that now arises over any recorded information that might have been used as supporting evidence We might also note that the death penalty was abolished in the United Kingdom partly because of the fallibility of the verdicts that might lead to wrong convictions.

The area of sexual abuse is one which inevitably concerns therapists. There is continuing controversy over rape cases and cases of sexual abuse because of the problems associated with obtaining reliable evidence. There was a time when victims of abuse were unlikely to be believed. This led to a great deal of protest and then to an unfortunate requirement that all those complaining of abuse must be believed so that public figures who might have been the subject of fantasies of all sorts as well as possible perpetrators of abuse have been investigated on very flimsy evidence or one person's word. British police have recently carried out wrongful and harmful investigations, which amounted to persecution. The indiscriminate culture of 'You must believe the complainant no matter what the case' has been discredited. This is one situation where certainty has been shown to have no place. The whole area of memory and of anger and hurt is sometimes more suited to the consulting room than the court room.

Uncertainty in fiction

Certainty can be harmful in the public and private spheres. Uncertainty is also problematic and can arouse fear. In *The Reluctant Fundamentalist* (2007), Mohsin Hamid, creates the sense of threat that accompanies uncertainty and relates to our animal nature. Changez, the man who is talking to the reader and to the American man in a café in Lahore, notes that the American is looking nervously around him. He is in a strange place and is behaving like an animal in strange surroundings. The lights go out because the electricity supply is variable and the American leaps to his feet. He brings to mind the behaviour of an animal that has ventured too far from its lair and is now in unfamiliar surroundings uncertain whether it is predator or prey (2007: 35)!

Hamid shows great skill in the way he moves the reader from one kind of uncertainty to another. Changez narrates the story of his time in New York where he was clearly out of place and yet he managed to achieve great success with the firm for which he works. Hamid has made it a firm which values other companies for purchases and sales and the reader is shown that valuing companies in this monetary and profit-motivated way can do much harm. In other words, it has a parasitic role and its decisions, we are told, make a great positive or negative difference to the employees. For a while though Changez is willing to shine as he finds that he is very good at this work. He begins to feel at home in New York and feels as though he can replace the dead lover of Erica. Then the Twin Towers are destroyed and the foundations of his new life begin to crumble. Hamid uses the impact of the bombing as an image of the way in which we all learned that what had appeared solid and safe could be toppled.

At this point the sense of threat in the novel comes closer to the surface. The American has been alarmed by the bats which are swooping low at dusk in Lahore but there is something much more disturbing in Changez's politeness and consideration even while he confesses how he rejoiced at the destruction of the Twin Towers and how much he cared about the invasion of Afghanistan. The tone of his narrative is polite but there is a mocking undertone when he explains the customs of the city and particularly of its food and drink. He orders dinner for the American who is put into the position of the naïve foreigner at his mercy. Changez's description of the food available in the market is significant. It is all meat, from an era 'before man's knowledge of cholesterol made him fearful of his prey ... These, Sir, are predatory delicacies imbued with a hint of wanton abandon'. He links this directly with the position of Pakistan and the resentment it causes:

> For we were not always burdened by debt, dependent on foreign aid and handouts. In the stories we tell of ourselves we were not the crazed and destitute radicals you see on your television channels but rather saints and poets and – yes – conquering kings.
>
> (2007: 115–16)

For a reader, the effect of Hamid's polite insistence is to emphasise unease and vulnerability. It also emphasises uncertainty. The American would prefer to go back to his hotel to eat but Changez will not have it and orders the predatory meal. In all this he is being a good and welcoming host but his behaviour seems intended to suggest some obscure threat behind it. Changez's narrative also shows the uncertainty engendered by being a stranger in a foreign land. At first in America he is welcomed and experiences great success in the terms of the Americans he meets but this is followed by disillusionment as he comes to understand what effect his work in saving or damning companies and therefore their workers is having on some of the poorer people.

The most interesting disillusionment that Changez experiences is in his love for the American woman, Erica. This at first went well but he discovered that she had lost a lover named Chris who had died. She was unable to allow the man from a different culture to replace Chris and she suffered from an underlying mental illness which attached itself to this loss. Once Changez suggested that she should imagine that he was Chris and this enabled them to make love successfully but it left her more ill than before and left him feeling guilty. He says that she was suffering from nostalgia but he is left not knowing how he could help her. He sees that he could not pretend to be a new Chris, or a genuine American. This becomes the one certainty that he has. He must live with not knowing what happens to Erica or what exactly made her unable to move on.

The novel is about uncertainty rushing in when the tide of certainty withdraws. Changez is employed in New York by a company that assesses the value of other companies. He is very good at this but he is taken in by the positive valuation that he receives for himself. Of course, it is conditional and when he is profoundly distracted by the India–Pakistan war, as well as the hostility of America towards Muslims, he has to re-evaluate. He is also taken in by Erica whom he loves and who, like the West as a whole is not able to love him because she has a dead lover whom she cannot abandon. To Changez, the West is obsessed with what is already dead. His story demonstrates that relying on the Western world is not secure and he suffers a great deal from forming his belief that he has become an American business man with a beautiful American girl friend. His certainties are eroded and he spends an evening showing the American stranger how much he has been hurt by the erosion of his beliefs. The 'reluctance' of the title of the novel refers perhaps to the optimism that he once had. He would no doubt have preferred to be able to continue with the life that he had expected in America. He was offered a job in the first place because he could get angry when the interviewer insulted him. Anger lurks beneath his smooth and courteous exterior and is one of the accompaniments of disillusionment.

The story of Changez and Erica reminds us that for all of us the one absolute certainty is death. The fear that Changez engenders is the fear that ordinary citizens may experience in relation to the threat to life posed by fundamentalists. For the everyday work of the therapist, attachment to dead or dying objects whether real or metaphorical needs to be addressed through working on the past. The fear of one's own dying and death is a subject that might also need to be addressed even though it will rarely be raised directly unless someone has a terminal diagnosis. Most clinicians are likely to see people whose close relatives have a terminal diagnosis but they need to remember that closeness to a dying relative or friend will also bring some thoughts about one's own death. This is difficult for the therapist who in this respect is in exactly the same position as the patient. It is, of course, one of the main reasons for requiring all therapists to have substantial personal therapy or analysis.

References

Bray, C. (2014) *A Song for Issy Bradley.* London: Hutchinson.

Green, A. (1981) 'Moral Narcissism' *International Journal of Psychoanalytic Psychotherapy* 8: 243–270.

Hamid, M. (2007) *The Reluctant Fundamentalist.* London: Penguin Books.

Lakoff, G. (2016) *Moral Politics.* Chicago, IL: University of Chicago Press.

Scott, L. (2018) 'From that dress to Yanny and Laurel:what tribal memes tell us about our fantasy and politics' *The Guardian* 30 May 2018.

Winnicott, W.D. (1963) 'The development of the capacity for concern' in Winnicott, D.W. (Ed.), *The Maturational Processes and Facilitating Environment.* London: Hogarth Press.

Chapter 3

Certainty in politics

> There is a holy mistaken zeal in politics as well as in religion. By persuading others, we convince ourselves.
>
> Junius, *Letter 35*, 1769

This letter by the eighteenth-century writer known as Junius refers to one of the main purposes of conviction: to support a position that may be in doubt. Politics, the science of the citizen, has always dealt with power. Aristotle wrote in the fourth century BC about the importance of the way in which a man should govern his slaves, his children and his wife. The term itself is derived from the Greek word *polis* meaning the people or the State. Unless it is modified (as it can be in, for example, 'domestic politics' or 'feminist politics'), the term generally refers to the way in which power is given and used in the State.

While the politics of any State are of great importance to the citizens, they are rarely the subject of an analytic session. Nevertheless, power relations in both public and personal affairs affect everyone and can be present in any narrative. This chapter will therefore look at the power issues in the dynamic psyche, how they are affected by the level of conviction in an individual. It will consider the processes involved in decision-making and in the distribution and use of power, especially within the individual. The psychodynamic model of the mind reminds us always that we deal with internal conflicts and tensions. Illustrations will be taken from elections in the UK and the United States and from the processes of environmentalism.

Conviction is at the heart of politics

The philosophical underpinning of political systems in the West will be considered from the questions about freedom raised by the logical positivists and existentialists of the last century and by such writers as Albert Camus and Harold Pinter. Simone de Beauvoir in *The Ethics of Ambiguity*

(1947) considered the limitations on freedom that each person faces and some of those ideas will help in understanding the urge for certainty and the constraints that it brings. *The Political Psyche* by Andrew Samuels (1993) will also be discussed, as it relates to the state of mind of the person suffering from existential angst and uncertainty. The passions of political strife are an expression of the emotional content of the certainty project.

Politics is also about promises. The politician has to assert certainty in what is often only a belief or a wish. Promises imply beliefs about the importance of the promises themselves and also about the reliability of the person making the promises. Put like this, certainty is very difficult to find in this context if it is to be based on evidence. In spite of this, the politician's task is to convince the electorate that his promises can certainly be fulfilled. As a result, the electorate is inclined to misinterpret an expression of intent and desire as promising a particular outcome. This of course is a phenomenon known in personal relationships as well.

Politics lends itself to assumptions that develop into beliefs. Traditionally the politician seeks to assert a set of beliefs and to persuade the people, to accept those beliefs without, necessarily, a basis in facts. Sometimes, of course, facts obtrude into political belief systems. An example of this would be the imposition of a reduction of income upon a section of the UK population, in some cases leading to poverty. This was the UK policy known as 'austerity' in the first decade of the twenty-first century. The stated rationale behind austerity was the need to 'balance the books'. The former British Prime Minister, Margaret Thatcher (in power 1979–1990), liked to look at the State as having much in common with the ordinary household and therefore the principle on which to base national economics was simple: live within your means. Of course, this principle is not new, nor is it limited to the UK.

Just what the 'means' of the State are and how they are derived is a matter of great concern and debate. One of the principles that Thatcher used to try to improve the economic position of the State was known as monetarism. For a time, the government tried to control the money supply in order to control prices, as Milton Friedman (1962) had proposed. In reality the targets that Thatcher set were often missed, and gradually monetarism was abandoned, although it had begun as a promising conviction. A main plank of conservatism in Western societies has remained as a conservative promise: to reduce debt and reduce the expenditure of the State. Unfortunately, if the State reduces the benefits that it pays to the most vulnerable, to the poor and to inadequate people, it will inevitably increase poverty and suffering. This brings anger and recrimination and gives comfort to opposing policies.

A certain amount of poverty in society may be accepted by the majority but there comes a point where the poverty can no longer be ignored. It becomes at least uncomfortable, even to those who are not suffering directly, and the political climate changes. Lack of jobs, and consequent lack of money and resources, contributed to the success of National Socialism in Germany in the 1930s and in the Referendum vote in 2016 for Britain to leave the European Union. In the United States this kind of motive led to the election of the populist leader Donald Trump as President.

Whatever the belief about the need for austerity, the political stance of the government will have an impact on the fate of all citizens. This area, as in many other areas where the State is acting, is determined by the moral position taken by politicians and thence by the electorate. This might remind us of the emotional content of morality. Those who feel that they are supporting the needy and vulnerable are naturally very strongly convinced that they are right. The person who is in favour of State benefits will see herself as altruistic and virtuous. In order to change this person's mind, there could be a need to find a narrative that enables a person to feel that the sense of virtue could lie in a different stance. Conservative thinkers in the US and Europe would be quick to claim morality for their own position, expecting everyone to make the most of his or her opportunities and not to be weakened by dependence on the State.

Certainty itself can be elevated into a virtue. In a speech at the Conservative Party conference in 1980, Margaret Thatcher usurped the title of Christopher Fry's play about a medieval witch-hunt, *The Lady's Not for Burning*. At the same time, she used the common belief that changing your mind is a bad thing: 'You turn if you want to – the lady's not for turning'. The proclamation reinforced the idea that a U-turn was something for others but not for a heroic leader. Thatcher had already become known as the Iron Lady, and the proclamation was warmly received with a standing ovation: she was effectively approved for not changing her mind.

Therapist U-turns

Therapists like certainty as much as anyone else. Patrick Casement altered this setting for some of us when he wrote *Learning from our Mistakes* (2002) to examine the value of the therapist's learning from getting it wrong. He reminds us that Freud identified ways that enable us to fend off any idea of being wrong as well as setting an example in his own work of being willing to change his mind. Freud told analysts that the response to an interpretation would not necessarily tell them that the interpretation is wrong. This is the phenomenon of 'Resistance'.

Resistance is a wonderful concept, because an analyst (or anyone else) who loves his own view of the situation can dismiss any counter-argument as resistance. Because it is a respectable theoretical and clinical concept, the label can enable an analyst to maintain arrogant, intrusive or even abusive beliefs. Casement's book lays out ways in which an analyst needs to be willing to try to identify with the patient. By doing so she can come to an understanding of what she has either got wrong or at least not yet understood.

Formation of political beliefs: patriotism and nationalism

Political convictions grow from childhood. What we call common sense is only a set of prejudices and beliefs acquired from teachers and authority figures usually by the end of schooling. Political beliefs generally are also passed down from parents. However, there is always the potential for rebellion although this may be passed through and laid aside by the time adulthood is reached.

In addition to learned beliefs, projection is a very important mechanism in politics and lends itself particularly well to our wish for certainty. Followers see in a leader the qualities and characteristics that they would most like to find in themselves. No wonder he or she is given leeway before supporters will find him or her to have been wrong. At the time of writing in the early twenty-first century, we have at least three stories going on which demonstrate the power of projection, where people believe that the leader is right. Two very charismatic leaders in the United States and Russia have fed on patriotism and the people's wish to form a successful group separated from others. Both have a devoted train of followers who accept whatever the leader does and manage to fit even the most transgressive behaviour into an accepted narrative.

When I meet Russians in the clinical space, there is often no discussion of the political situation in Russia, but the mere fact that, in spite of all the difficulties here, they have chosen to live in the UK indicates to me that all of them have had even greater perceived problems back in Russia.

President Trump in the United States seems to be very similar to President Putin in that he was elected on the basis of making his country 'great again'. He used the idea of inclusion. Those who voted for him would join him in that project. As always, economics entered the picture. At the time of his rise to power, the United States was going through a time of economic distress, particularly in manufacturing, where it was suffering from competition from the rest of the world, particularly China. His election was a close-run thing, with the electoral college system providing his triumph although he received slightly fewer of the popular votes than his rival. The rival candidate, Hillary Clinton, received about 2.9 million more votes than Donald Trump nationwide, a margin of 2.1%, but Trump won 30 States with a total of 306 electors, or 57% of the 538 available.

With a narrow success of this sort, it would be reasonable to think that at least some of President Trump's supporters would be open to changing their minds when they saw how he behaved in office and that the price of his putting America first, as he had clearly promised to do, was to endanger international statesmanship. The abandonment of efforts to combat climate change and persecution of minorities, particularly Muslims, Latinos and Lesbian, Gay and Trans minorities seem to be accepted by the majority of his supporters as Trump doing what he said he would do. 'Vox pop' interviews show that his supporters see him as their champion, possessing all the qualities that they themselves wish to have. He also has the power of the richest nation on Earth, so that he can go around the world saying and doing what he likes.

In the UK, a similar wave of populism attended the public appearances of Nigel Farage, who founded a political party, the UK Independence Party (UKIP) on his dislike of Britain's membership of the European Union. Like Trump, he proposed to make his country great again and like Trump he offered absolute certainty about how to do it. The two men seem to get on well together, sharing self-confidence and certainty about their policies. Farage in common with other populist leaders ignored ordinary norms of responsibility or courtesy and this seems to excite his followers. They too can be right without doubts. He took the personal benefits of his own elected membership of the European Parliament with great enthusiasm while energetically talking it down at home. Fear of the success of his new party led the Conservative Party, one of the main parties in the UK being challenged by UKIP, to take up Farage's policy and offer a referendum in 2016 on the subject of leaving the European Union. The result was as close as the vote that elected Trump: the UK voted to leave the European Union by 51.9% to 48.1%, a margin of 3.8%. This created the most painful divisions in the country since the Civil War of the seventeenth century.

As time passed between the vote for Britain to leave the European Union and the reality of leaving, there was evidence, day by day, of the risks in what had been decided. Economists and scientists in particular were opposed to what looked to them like a dangerous undertaking but again the people who voted for this were not willing to change their minds. Why not? The reasons for this level of certainty are many and complex.

One of the strongest reasons may be unconscious. Nigel Farage, a right wing populist in the UK, was seen as a breezy and bluff individual who invited his followers to feel part of a chosen brigade of patriots. Farage had himself photographed guffawing, with a beer in his hand, emphasizing that he is just an ordinary person who might be met in any bar. His views have been called 'xenophobic' and 'jingoistic' by opponents but seem to have expressed what many secretly felt. This relates to one of Freud's main arguments in *Group Psychology and the Analysis of the Ego* (1921). Being a member of a group means that the restraints that an individual puts on him or herself are lifted. In other words, the group takes on norms and standards that may be much less civilised than those that the individual would wish to acknowledge for herself, but because everyone else in the group is accepting the group norms, each individual feels that she can too. This process is powerful and may have contributed to the excesses of Nazi Germany in the 1930s to 40s.

Staying convinced

Freud's theory goes some way to explaining the support enjoyed by populist leaders in Europe and the United States of the early twenty-first century. None of these movements has come close to Nazi excesses but the danger of excess is always there. Once someone is committed to a group, we cannot rely on him to judge his own behaviour by the standards that he would have used if left to himself. Quoting with approval Le Bon's 'deservedly famous work' (Le Bon 1920), Freud (1921) writes:

> There are certain ideas and feelings which do not come into being, or do not transform themselves into acts except in the case of individuals forming a group. The psychological group is a provisional being formed of heterogeneous elements, which for a moment are combined, exactly as the cells which constitute a living body form by their reunion a new being which displays characteristics very different from those possessed by each of the cells singly.

(29)

This hypothesis would explain the difficulty of convincing anyone that he or she has been wrong in choosing to vote one way or the other. The only circumstances in which we might expect such a change to take place would be if there is known to be sufficient support for the new point of view. Formation of a new group would have to seem possible. Newly formed political parties rarely seem to manage to achieve this level of support and we have to suppose that there is not usually enough mass to enable the necessary chain reaction to begin.

Sometimes new political parties can provide both a sense of belonging and the emotional charge of promoting new ideas. The formation of the British Labour Party through the action of the Trade Union Congress in 1900 was an agglomeration of political groups and movements that traced their origins to the nineteenth century. The same is true of the Liberal Party in the UK. The failure of the Social Democratic Party (SDP) to survive after its foundation in the UK in 1981 is further evidence of this need to offer people a feeling of joining a group with enough emotional conviction to provide a sense of belonging. By joining with the Liberal Party in 1988 to form the Liberal Democrats, the founders of the SDP hoped that they might achieve this level of conviction, but at the time of writing the Liberal Democrats have yet to form a government; the closest they have come to power is as part of a coalition with the Conservative Party between 2010 and 2015. The search for critical mass was not successful.

Feminist conviction

What applies at this macro level also applies to the internal mind-set of an individual. It is here where the determination to join or oppose a group is formed. Some of these group memberships become part of the individual's identity and are not likely to change. Feminism is an example of the position that a woman might take up. Although being 'a feminist' might seem a step too far for the average woman in Western society, most women there would expect to have the freedom to work and to succeed in work at any level according to their ability. They would expect to be free to choose when and with whom to have sexual relations. They would expect to be able to vote and to participate in politics on an equal footing with men. All of this is of course unavailable in some societies and might sometimes be at risk in any culture.

Adopting the title of 'feminist' means a commitment that goes beyond taking these freedoms for granted. In order to think that she needs to become a feminist, a woman must be convinced at a level of certainty that women risk losing these basic rights or do not yet have them. A woman who proclaims her feminism is likely to encounter antagonism, which often strengthens conviction making it all the more resilient and sometimes aggressive.

The role of hostility may be to push an individual either to give in or to dig in. Many psychoanalytic theorists have been exercised by the need to explain aggression. Freudian theorists relate aggression to the drives and see it as a necessary component of the libido. Repression, or frustration of libidinal impulses, may lead to aggression. The Oedipus complex is helpful in understanding this process. The child loves and wants the parent of the opposite sex all to him or herself. The same-sex parent stands in the way of the realisation of these desires and aggression develops in response to the feeling of rivalry. The social response theories of aggression emphasise the extent to which a child learns behaviour from watching his parents. Children observe the importance of gender and will be trying to work out how to be a man or a woman. According to this perspective, we must look to the models that were available to the child to understand the response that any individual will show to frustration.

Aggression is destructive. Everyone knows this, so most people feel the need to be right in order to be justified in showing it, especially to those closest who often receive the most vicious attacks. For this reason alone, we can see the need for certainty that the aggression is justified. Unwarranted certainty is frequently the result. Of course, the reasons for a display of aggression are many but we know that its existence is continuous throughout human history, both at a group and individual level. It shows us that the primary nature of certainty is emotional. The patient who tells me that he lost his temper and shouted at his partner is telling me that for that moment, at least, he was convinced that she was wrong and he was right. This feeling is part of a pattern with its roots in infancy. The infant has no capacity for rational consideration but reacts against anything that seems to threaten his possession of the source of safety and food, which is usually his mother. There is instead an immediate reaction that in infantile terms is aggressive.

After an aggressive attack the conviction of having a just cause may harden into a certainty, which is resistant to change.

Studies of change

So far this chapter has considered what pulls a person to one side of a public debate and locks him in conviction. Going back to the question of how people can change, we are confronted with two theories of mental development. Park (2015) has described two explanations as the 'entity theory' and the 'incremental theory'.

According to the entity theory the process of development can work only with what is there by genetic inheritance and is therefore limited. On the other hand, according to the incremental theory, much more depends on the early environment and change is therefore possible at a more fundamental level. Going back to the neurologists we find that the accepted view now is that there is a considerable degree of plasticity in the brain. Young people are much more able to change the structure of the brain, through experience, than older people. But even into old age there is some possibility of changing the structure of the brain by developing new neural pathways. Studies of spatial learning for example have indicated that there are structural changes in the neural pathways when new spatial information is acquired (Keller & Just 2016).

If this means that habitual ways of thinking can be changed by new experiences and new cognitive approaches to the world view, there is much reason for the therapist not to accept too easily the patient's view that 'this is just the way I am'. Deep change is difficult to bring about through cognitive means and in spite of the success of Cognitive Behavioural Therapy in helping with some emotional difficulties, it does not yet seem to be able to bring about profound and lasting change to deeply held convictions.

Experience however can bring change even in political orientation. The UK's experience of leaving the European Union has brought unprecedented passion, anger and hatred to politics at the national and also domestic level. Yet the events as they have unfolded have led to respected politicians of various ages, including some senior and revered members of parliament, leaving the political party to which they have belonged for the whole of their political lives. In doing so they risked their jobs and their status. This group of politicians have not at the time of writing found a clear new policy for themselves but they were clearly capable of great and uncomfortable change.

Confirmation bias

Internal and external politics depend on the basis on which choices are made. Writers like the theologian James Packer (1958) have considered the authority on which religious fundamentalism in Christianity is based. Fundamentalism in politics is at least as important to all those of us living in a democracy and is relevant to the therapist working with the internal dynamics of the individual. Man as a tribal animal looks for a leader or in some cases, seeks to be a leader himself. When a leader presents him or herself with sufficient confidence and enough charisma many people will seize on this with relief. We can see this in the consulting room where the therapist is the one who is supposed to know.

Gerry came to see a therapist and described in the first session her difficulties with her line manager. 'She never gives me any feedback. I never know how I am doing or what she thinks about me'. The therapist understood that there is a genuine difficulty at work and that there is a probing of the way therapy might work as well. Gerry will want to be told how she should think by the authority she has vested in the therapist. Gerry demonstrates that we are talking about both men and women seeking to find a leader to relieve us of the need to make up our own minds.

An interesting experiment by an American political scientist, Philip Tetlock (2002), demonstrated the social component of our adherence to an authority once chosen. Subjects were given a case to judge and were told either that they would have to justify the conclusion that they reached or were just asked to made the decision with no mention of anyone else paying attention. When people know that they will have to explain themselves they are more inclined to think systematically and rationally. Their thinking, Tetlock found, fell into two categories: the 'exploratory', which sought to review the possibilities in a more or less open way, and the 'confirmatory', in which the intention seemed to be to support decisions that had already been made. These findings confirm the widespread impression that people use social media to support opinions that they have already formed. Some research into confirmation bias has been carried out by cognitive psychologists such as Mercier and Sperber (2011) who were looking at the motivation behind wishing to win an argument. They concluded that most of the arguments that are used in academic papers are designed to persuade and convince rather than to seek for truth. As Jonathan Haidt (2013) puts it 'Intuition comes first and Reasoning comes second'.

We ask 'Can I believe it?' when we want to believe something but 'Must I believe it?' when we don't want to believe. The answer is almost always yes to the first question and no to the second.

(Haidt 2013: 107)

For a politician the question is therefore how to make all her promises so desirable that the questions are in the form of, 'Can I believe it?'. She can then lead voters to ask themselves whether they can allow the greed or the optimism or whatever is being activated to predominate or whether they have to be as dubious as the second type of question would require. Haidt also describes some work by Westen et al. (2006) in which he studied brain activation in an MRI scanner of subjects who were told something negative about their favoured political candidate. They were then told that he had changed his policy to something more ethical and desirable. The important observation was that there was a dopamine 'hit' when the relief came and there was no need to believe the negative message any more. If this sort of confirmation of the hopes and desires leads to a physical reward similar to that experienced with drugs like heroin, the person who is trying to argue for something undesirable, like higher taxes to pay for social services, is going to have a very hard time.

Motivation to change your mind

The question for a therapist is always to consider how to avoid any temptation simply to provide positive dopamine-evoking words. Gerry says she wants feedback, but there is a question for her therapist to resolve. Will she accept any feedback that differs from her belief and, not only her belief, but her wish?

Gerry begins to talk about her difficulties with her partner Joanna. She says that they are often so angry with each other that they don't speak. She describes the way they communicate through the statue of a dog that they keep on a shelf. With some hesitation she describes a very intimate habit they both have of addressing the dog as 'Mr Rough'. One will say to the other 'Mr Rough thinks that we should go to the pub this evening'. The other would than respond 'Mr Rough doesn't understand how tired I am. He needs to pay some attention to my feelings for once'.

The therapist heard this with some discomfort and after hearing about several exchanges of this sort wanted to say something about the difficulty of indirect communication. She said, 'You both seem to find it difficult to speak directly to each other'. Gerry was immediately angry and retorted, 'I've just told you something really personal and all you can do is make it sound silly'. The therapist felt that this was a very delicate moment. She had not thought that it was silly but that it set up an elaborate routine that avoided direct confrontation. On the other hand she could see that it enabled them to say things to each other which might have been difficult otherwise. She also thought that there must be some significance in calling the dog 'Mr Rough' as though the two of them wanted a ruthless authority to adjudicate in their arguments. Maybe they also wanted the energy and aggression of a man even though neither of them would have wanted an actual man.

Confrontation is difficult for most people who are not unduly paranoid and the therapist at this point could see some parallel process in that she was hesitating to confront Gerry. Out of all these thoughts she had to choose what might be helpful or take the safe course of waiting and giving herself time to consider further. She decided to comment on the process by saying that she was finding herself anxious about saying something that would be hurtful, just as Gerry herself might have been about what she wanted to say to Joanna. Gerry agreed that she did find confrontation difficult. 'Well' said the therapist, 'you just took the risk of confronting me and we still seem to be talking to each other'. Gerry said nothing. But the temperature of the session dropped and there was a calmer period in which she talked about a good time that she had experienced with Joanna the previous week when they had both gone to a film together.

In doing this the therapist was allowing the kind of return from a negative experience that Westen et al. (2006) had found to give an experience of pleasure to the brain. This sort of repetition leaves the way open to some sort of change if the therapist can then understand it. The change was gradual and came across in small hints over the next weeks and months. What had happened was that Gerry had found that pleasure could be associated with risking a confrontation with her therapist. In this way the process of confirmation bias was disrupted and the patient was led to accept a message that began a process of change.

Freud might have told us that we should pay attention to what the patient wants. This therapist was thinking about the presenting problem and the difficulties that Gerry was describing at work. From the 1960s the possibility of the transfer of training from one specific piece of learning to others that are similar has been an important aspect of educational theory where everyone is concerned with change and the ways in which it can occur. D. H. Holding (1965) published his influential manual on the principles of training which conveyed the importance of specific help in how to transfer knowledge from one sphere into another. Therapists have to consider the process by which this can be made useful to patients. Since the process of any psychodynamic therapy involves establishing links from the conscious to the unconscious parts of the mind and thence back into consciousness, therapists will be well used to commenting on connections that the patient might not have recognised. This process is itself crucial to unfixing the damaging certainty of old patterns, making way for new possibilities.

All of this can convince us that work on the relationship with her partner will help Gerry with her problems at work as long as the therapist makes the connections in some way. Gerry had said that she did not know what her manager thinks of her and she wanted feedback. This is a beginning. They will both have to find out what Gerry herself thinks about her performance and what she fears. This of course is easier said than done. Some therapists might plunge straight in and ask her what she thinks the manager might have said. Others might try to deduce it from what she says about Joanna. For example, as she begins to talk to her more about what is going on between them, she begins to complain about Joanna's selfishness. She says, 'I know that I can be annoying but it's mostly when I can't make up my mind. What's so bad about that? She just can't wait for me to decide'. There is a pause and then she adds, 'I suppose that could be a bit annoying'. The therapist feels some relief at this sign of Gerry's ability to arrive at her own challenge. The therapist here might risk asking her whether this useful understanding gives her any hint about what her manager might say.

Considering the ways in which the work with Gerry might go takes us away from the challenges of the public sphere even though some of the mental processes are the same. One of the factors that seems to operate in the political sphere is the desire that people feel to be free of normal civilised inhibitions. A phenomenon of the early twenty-first century has been the development of large-scale use of social media. Politicians have revealed that they have been severely abused by anonymous posts on major current social media, such as Twitter and Facebook. A writer like Sayeeda Warsi (2017) in her defence of British Muslims, *The Enemy Within: A Tale of Muslim Britain* is far from sensationalist. But she mentions in passing the way in which she had been treated on line. She quotes a survey of Muslims in Birmingham by a Member of Parliament in 2015 which showed that 87% of those questioned said that they or someone they knew had experienced 'Islamophobia'.

There is much certainty in racial hatred. Islamophobia is a term that should mean 'fear of the religion of Islam'. It has usually been popularly taken to mean hatred of Muslims. That has hardened into a certainty and is used as a criticism of any language or behaviour that is opposed to Muslims or Islam. There is of course fear of the violent forms of jihad and fear leads to hatred, as the whole theory of paranoia teaches us. The process by which fear is transformed into hatred is important both socially and within the individual. Freud (1911) analysed the autobiography of Dr Daniel Schreber, showing the steps by which Schreber transformed fear of his own homosexuality into hatred. 'I (a man) love him (a man)' was unacceptable and became the opposite: 'I do not love him, I hate him'. This feeling of hate cannot stand on its own and has to be justified. It becomes 'I hate him because he persecutes me' (Freud 1911: 201).

Once the negative feelings have begun to hold sway in an individual we can see that there is some pleasure in the release of the feelings in an expression of hatred. The Internet provides an unprecedented opportunity to express hatred without being identified and therefore without taking the consequences.

Is there any way in which convictions can be tackled since they are often hidden? Therapists know that they need to identify underlying convictions that lead to what is unbearable and has to be evacuated vehemently and sometimes even violently. In *The Confidence Game* (2016) Maria Kornikova studies the methods used by confidence tricksters of all sorts to identify a 'mark' or victim in order to deceive him or her and escape without being caught. She describes the fairly predictable techniques by which Spiritualist mediums learn about an individual's life from friends, the Internet and chance encounters. The mark might be chosen after such information has been acquired. Using facts about their life will fill the mark with conviction that the medium knows what she is talking about and is to be trusted. These fraudsters are also very good at interpreting appearance, body language and behaviour, let alone words and narrative to understand the person in front of them. Therapists of course use some of the same techniques when listening to patients and can reinforce their position as 'the one who is supposed to know' and in fact become the one who does know. The difference of course is that the therapist uses the information and understanding for the benefit of the patient.

Carol was a history graduate who began her working life as a teacher in a comprehensive secondary school. She was a quiet, somewhat reserved woman, and she found class control very difficult. Each day she had to pluck up her courage to get up and go to work. She had taken a Diploma in Education but had found the practical experience of teaching a great strain. She passed the placement to her own surprise and had found herself trying to control a class of 35 young people, many of whom had little or no interest in the unification of Germany. She married Edward, a Maths graduate who was an accountant. He didn't seem very interested in Carol's problems, just saying that if she didn't like what she was doing she should change jobs. Carol had a friend Mel, who worked for the Samaritans and said, 'Why don't you train to be a counsellor? You work with one person at a time and you don't have to say much'. Carol liked the sound of that and began to think that maybe she would like to see a counsellor herself to talk about her growing difficulties with her marriage.

Carol cut her teaching hours to part-time and travelled to London to train as a counsellor. She found that she greatly enjoyed the new way of thinking about history and its place in each person's life. She enjoyed the reading and the discussions with her fellow trainees. She learnt to understand a whole new way of talking and thinking. She liked the new emphasis on not knowing. She had recently spent three years of an undergraduate degree course trying to get answers right and trying to remember everything she read. Here in her new world she was told that there were rarely 'right answers'. She found that a great relief. On the other hand, her existing training had trained her to seek certainty. Even her understanding of historical relativity had not entirely changed her interest in facts.

When she qualified as a counsellor, Carol found herself so interested in the theory that she wanted to train as a psychotherapist. She obtained a place in a course and began to work with a new student group. This group contained a trainee called Mandy. Carol found everything about Mandy difficult. She was full of ideas about how people would respond to being loved by the therapist. Carol was moved to fury by what she perceived to be intellectual slackness. She accused the whole group of pandering to this weakness and told her therapist that she wanted to leave.

The next weeks were painful for Carol who had felt let down by the training, which was not valuing her academic ability. With the help of her therapist she began to realise that Mandy was giving her the opportunity to learn to respect the views of others even when they bring in a framework that is very different from one's own. Over time she discovered that there was a rationale for Mandy's approach and that Mandy was willing to listen to Carol's ideas once they had argued with each other a few times. Each of them discovered that their own perspective was deepened by adopting and adapting something from the other. If politics is the art of the possible, as Otto von Bismarck said, expectations of therapy also must also take account of what each therapist is capable of doing. Therapists may make use of each other's ideas and will inevitably adopt some beliefs with the strength of convictions.

With all this adoption of strong positions, how is a therapist to shake a patient's profound convictions that she will not let go? In the case of the confidence tricksters described by Kornikova, disillusionment is often brought about by loss. If the deception involves loss of money, which it almost always does, the individual becomes aware of having been deceived. One woman was persuaded by a clairvoyant to hand over all her savings (that amounted to $27,000), which the clairvoyant promised to keep safe for her to avoid some misadventure. This would demonstrate her trust in the clairvoyant. The woman did this but afterwards was overcome by misgivings and tried to get the money back. Needless to say, there was no reply when she tried to telephone or e-mail or even turn up on the doorstep and the cheque had already been cashed.

In politics as in most other spheres of human life, money is a powerful motivator. Running for the American presidency in 1992, Bill Clinton adopted the phrase, 'It's the economy, stupid' as a key message that would win the election. In his definition of politics in *The Political Psyche* Andrew Samuels (1993) speaks of the struggles over power and the way that power relates to 'the organisation and distribution of resources' particularly economic resources (1993: 3). Money pulls people into action. However, money does not have power to change beliefs.

In considering the importance of conviction in human life there is no avoiding the importance of money, but it has to be relegated to its subordinate role. It is only a symbol, which means different things for each person. In moving from person to person it becomes a power. What kind of power or control does each person want? In this lies the root of the individual's beliefs about the world in which she lives. Only by attempting to grasp the reason for the underlying convictions can a therapist hope to understand the individual's political state, both internally and externally, so that she can hope to help change it.

References

Casement, P. (2002) *Learning from Our Mistakes*. London: Routledge.

de Beauvoir, S. (1947) *The Ethics of Ambiguity*, trans (1948) by Bernard Frechtman. New York: Citadel Press.

Freud, S. (1911) 'Psyhoanalytic Notes on an Autobiographical Account of a Case of Paranoia' *S.E.* 12: 1–82.

Freud, S. (1921) *Group Psychology and the Analysis of the Ego*, The Standard Edition of the *Complete Psychological Works of Sigmund Freud*, Volume XVIII. London: Hogarth Press.

Friedman, M. (1962) *Capitalism and Freedom*. Chicago: University of Chicago Press.

Haidt, J. (2013) *The Righteous Mind*. Harmondsworth: Penguin Books.

Holding, D.H. (1965) *Principles of Training*. Oxford: Pergamon Press.

Junius. (1772) *Letters of Junius*. London: Henry Sampson Woodfall.

Keller, T.A. & Just, M.A. (2016) 'Structural and functional neuroplasticity in human learning of spatial routes' *NeuroImage* 125: 256–266.

Kornikova, M. (2016) *The Confidence Game*. New York: Viking Press.

Le Bon, G. (1920) *The Crowd: A Study of the Popular Mind*. London: Fisher Unwin, 12th. Impression.

Mercier, H. & Sperber, D. (2011) 'Why do humans reason?' *Behavioural and Brain Sciences* 34: 57–74.

Packer, J.I. (1958) *Fundamentalism and the Word of God*. London: Inter-Varsity Fellowship.

Park, D. (2015) 'Time to move on? when entity theorists perform better than incremental theorists' *Personality and Social Psychology Bulletin* 41(5): 736–748.

Samuels, A. (1993) *The Political Psyche*. London: Routledge.

Tetlock, P.E. (2002) 'Social functionalist frameworks for judgment and choice: intuitive politicians, theologians and prosecutors' *Psychological Review* 109: 451–457.

Warsi, S. (2017) *The Enemy Within: A Tale of Muslim Britain*. Harmondsworth: Penguin Books.

Westen, D., Blagov, P.S., Harenski, K., Kilts, C., & Hamann, S. (2006) 'Neural bases of motivated reasoning' *Journal of Cognitive Neuroscience* 18: 1947–1958.

Chapter 4

Certainty in religion

There lives more faith in honest doubt,
Believe me, than in half the creeds.
                    Alfred, Lord Tennyson,
                    In Memoriam A. H. H., 1833

The Victorian poet Alfred Tennyson lived in a time of public religious certainty but also of scientific and social questioning. Deeply affected by the sudden death at the age of 22 of his closest friend Arthur Henry Hallam, Tennyson pointed in *In Memoriam A. H. H.* (Roberts 2009) to the profoundly painful experience of religious doubt but emphasised that it can enable more well-founded certainty in the longer term. Belief is a matter of choice. Yet no-one thinks he is choosing from a range of competitive assertions. Religions do not expect their adherents to arrive at truth by a process of reasoning based on an assessment of evidence. Since they deal with the transcendental, they tend more often to demand that their adherents hold convictions based on faith – there is one right answer. These convictions are usually derived from authorities, often parents or their representatives. The position is complicated because religion is often confused with culture and objections to cultural practices are met as though they were objections to a religious faith.

Dealing with convictions that share some of the characteristics of religion is the usual work of psychotherapy. On the other hand, religion that gives comfort or hope but does no apparent harm need not be our concern. The nature and aetiology of religion are relevant to all sorts of convictions and may need to be addressed in therapeutic work since such statements as, 'That's just the way I am' and 'I can't do that' can take on all the unchallengeable numinosity of a religious declaration. Such dogmatic statements may serve the purpose of removing all possibility of there being a choice.

Some of the difficult positions held in the face of religious conviction are discussed by Sayeeda Warsi (2017). She focused on the treatment of Muslims in the United Kingdom in the twentieth and twenty-first centuries. Her book therefore looks at the social meaning of a religion and she encourages thought about the social implications of professing a religious belief, which is by no means monolithic but which is seen as such from the outside. Of course, it is not surprising that the rest of the country and the world blamed 'the Muslims' in general and the religion in particular for the tragic terrorist attacks on the World Trade Center and elsewhere. Warsi accepts that this view is not surprising but she asks us all to think about it: 'Civil war, foreign invasions, conflict, upheavals, strife in countries around the world are shared problems ... These are our problems to solve' (2017: 90). She adds her view of one aspect of what causes fundamentalism:

> In developed countries where discrimination and disengagement are prevalent, terrorism is too. These too are our problems to fix ... to create more equal, more engaged communities where all feel as if they have equal access to opportunity and feel as if they belong.
>
> (Warsi 2017: 90)

Warsi does not in any way minimise the importance of her faith to her personally or to other British citizens. But she does point out that terrorist attacks have been a problem for ordinary British Muslims because they have led to blaming all Muslims. This in turn has led to attacks based on hatred of the religion itself while the terrorists have mostly appeared to be ignorant of the principles of the religion whose name they were using. In evidence to the investigation, *Roots of Violent Radicalisation*, by the Home Affairs Committee of the House of Commons of the UK Parliament, the Home Office admitted that:

> There is no standard profile of a terrorist and no single pathway or route that a terrorist takes to becoming involved in a terrorist organisation.
>
> (Home Affairs Committee, 2012, Evidence page ev 88, section 1.3)

Warsi argues that fundamentalism is not the same as terrorism. She points out that there are fundamentalists in all religions and that not all fundamentalists are terrorists and not all terrorists are religious. She is arguing instead that fundamentalism is a state of mind that occurs for all sorts of reasons but is not equivalent to terrorism. She is convinced that the roots of fundamentalism of a harmful sort lie in areas of psychology and sociology but that religion may provide the sense of belonging and of contributing to something memorable that people seek:

> What inspires the most lethal terrorists in the world today is not the Qr'an or religious teaching as much as a thrilling cause and call to action that promises glory and esteem in the eyes of friends.
>
> (Atran 2014)

When it comes to intolerance, Warsi is clear that it is a widespread human failing. Her own parents made it clear that there are many ways to practise Islam. She became aware of sectarianism and intolerance among the different versions of Islam, particularly the strife between Shia and Sunni Muslims which is as deadly at times as the Roman Catholic versus Protestant versions of Christianity.

We are brought back to the same question as always. What is the satisfaction to be obtained from a passionate conviction excluding all those who do not share the same beliefs? In fact, this formulation of the question seems to lead back towards one aspect of the reason for it. Human beings are tribal animals. Like baboons or wild dogs, we live in packs and the males are hard-wired to fight other packs that threaten to steal the food source and have sex with the females. Football fans are noted for their tribal behaviour towards their opponents, with Macgrath (2016) instancing as a prime example a chant: 'Bournemouth [or other team name] boys, we are here. Fuck your women, drink your beer' (Macgrath 2016: 60). Females join in the violence either directly or by encouraging it; this relates to their need to protect their babies and young offspring. A series of programmes on BBC in July 2019 called *Serengeti* demonstrated the importance of the need of lionesses to fight off lions who did not father the offspring. A powerful male lion joining new pride kills any existing cubs in order to bring the females into oestrus and to be certain that he fathered the young ones that he will in future protect. His own genes will predominate.

Women and religious fundamentalism

Returning to the human species, many religions promote the treatment of women that seems to relate to our animal nature more than to any level of civilisation. Rules about the place of women have become one of the most damaging convictions of fundamentalism.

In many religious groups, women have been assigned a place that from the male point of view seems desirable. Women should be modest, subservient, domesticated and entirely faithful to the husband once married. This has been the position in all the major world religions, to a greater or lesser extent. Michael Arditti (2009) has written a moving novel, *The Enemy of the Good*, about the life of a woman living in North London with a Jewish mother. She becomes an Orthodox Jew in order to marry Zvi, who belongs to the Orthodox Jewish Hasidic movement called Lubavitch, subscribing to the most extreme version of what might appear as the exploitation of women.

Susannah chooses to submit herself to the regime in order to marry Zvi and takes pleasure in her conversion and sense of virtue. Her mother finds the strict practices observed in the sect alarming and thinks that her daughter has always been obsessional:

Susannah had always been an obsessive child keeping everything from the toys in her nursery to the towels in her bathroom in perfect order.

(2009: 169)

This sort of personality is likely to find the rigorous laws of a fundamentalist sect satisfying. Arditti shows the conversion as damaging in that Susannah is so sure that she is right that when her brother who is not a member of her sect helps their father to die when he is desperately ill and in pain, she reports him to the police and he serves a prison sentence. There can be little doubt that Arditti is showing that this sort of conviction can be a sort of prison in itself. He does not overtly condemn religious fundamentalism but he shows the pain that it can produce.

The title of Arditti's novel, *The Enemy of the Good*, refers to an Italian proverb quoted by Voltaire in his *Dictionaire Philosophique* of 1770. The complete form of the aphorism is: 'the best is the enemy of the good'. This title comments on the search for perfection in fundamentalism. In their quest for the absolute authority that can be obeyed without question, those who show fundamentalist traits are always seeking the possibility of perfection and in so doing they are missing a more ordinary virtue or what is actually good enough.

The psychiatrist Donald Winnicott identified the 'good enough' mother who can do what the infant needs partly because of the mother's own experience of being an infant. This is an adaptation of the mother to her baby, which must gradually fail as the infant's needs become so complex that she cannot fulfil them. In fact, Winnicott says, she needs to fail so that the infant can learn to manage the frustrations and disappointments of life:

> The good-enough mother ... starts off with an almost complete adaptation to her infant's needs, and, as time proceeds, she adapts less and less completely, gradually, according to the infant's growing ability to deal with her failure.
>
> (Winnicott 1974: 12)

The important qualification here is that the mother should fail gradually and bearably. A catastrophic failure will have an impact that resonates throughout life but the failure that comes from a loving and willing parent can be used in the service of development. Therapists will often see the dangers of a search for perfection but need to understand the reasons for that need. The perfect mother could never let her baby down or fail him. If that were possible, paradoxically, she would be failing her infant because he would not learn to deal with frustration in a safe environment.

Mother never lets go

A young American academic studying at a British university was unable to write up and finish his PhD. Harrison was caught in the not uncommon problem that he was not able to stop seeking further information, continuing the search for completeness even though his academic supervisor had told him that he was unlikely to add anything significant. Therapy seemed to be going nowhere and in fact the therapist began to think that it was only wasting valuable time that would be better spent in beginning the writing-up process. As the work continued and the sense of hopelessness increased, Harrison began to talk about the way he had felt about his mother. She was a hairdresser in his home town in the United States and was evidently immensely proud of him. His two older brothers had both gone to work in the motor manufacturing industry in the next town but he had gone to college.

Harrison felt extremely guilty, he said, because his mother had used most of her savings to send him to college where he obtained a degree summa cum laude and then came to the UK to work on a doctorate. He believed that through his achievement she was experiencing the nearest thing to the academic success that she herself had wanted. The therapist helped him to see that, through his delay in finishing his doctorate, he was expressing unwillingness to get his doctorate for his mother's benefit. He was angry with the expectation that he felt obliged to fulfil. He agreed with this but it did not seem to help. The therapist was bothered by his own wish that Harrison would get on and finish. Through this anxiety about his own role, the therapist came to understand that he thought Harrison was very bright and would write a very good dissertation. The therapist realised that it was the need for perfection that was stopping Harrison from getting on and writing what might turn out to be only a moderately good dissertation or even one that would be rejected for revisions and corrections. Harrison's fear was mixed up with his knowledge that his mother thought that he would be very successful but that his success so far had raised expectations, making the possibility that the expectations might not be fulfilled bitterer. He was desperate to be just one of the family, alongside his brothers.

As Harrison talked, he also discovered feelings that related to being the youngest son. He already knew that he had been a problem for his parents. When he was 14 his mother had told him that his father had wanted her to have an abortion as they could not afford a third child. She had refused because she was a Roman Catholic and the Church told her that abortion was a sin. His father, who was not a Roman Catholic, had left his mother before the birth. She took on extra work and they managed, although they were often on the edge of not having enough to eat. This helped him to understand the way his mother had idealised him. She had to be right about her decision to keep him even though it had threatened her own wellbeing and that of his two brothers. This had led to his mother's heightened expectations of her 'perfect little boy'. By telling him about this, she was showing that she was confident of his perfection. She expected that he would not have a problem with knowing this but would be able to support and comfort her and be grateful to her for keeping him alive.

Harrison had suffered from his mother's need to have been right and from her subsequent idealisation to make him perfect. Only after he had recognised these aspects of his relationship with her was he able to begin to understand her better and then to understand himself. The effect took time to achieve but after about six months he began to think that he would complete his dissertation for his own sake but could let his mother share in the success.

Religious change

Religious conviction can be narrow. It can be a form of narcissism: a person may be prepared to tolerate only the beliefs that he has chosen to suit his own projections. A broader, more tolerant perspective will help in interpersonal relations as well as in relations with the chosen deity.

What does this mean in practice? A broader humanity might mean a tolerance of different approaches to what 'god' means. When fundamentalism becomes problematic, it is at least partly because there is no possibility of seeing another point of view. Warsi describes her religious upbringing as teaching this kind of tolerance. Even though her parents had grown up with a strict observance of Islam and even though that continued in the mosque they were still able to let themselves be ruled by generosity:

> The teachings favoured in the local mosques we attended were both conservative and puritanical. Many of the cultural practices which my parents had grown up with were seen as unnecessary at best and forbidden at worst. This didn't seem to worry my parents …
>
> Our parents never taught us that a specific version of the faith was wrong, instead telling us that there were many ways to pray and worship, an upbringing opposite to divisive sectarianism which can be politically exploited and trigger deep hatred.
>
> (Warsi 2017: xxiii)

Of course, this sort of latitude may extend only to sects within a particular religion but in principle it could be extended to all religions as just different ways of worshipping. Such an attitude is rare and might abolish the need for fundamentalism – if fundamentalism were based on only one belief. Warsi's argument supports a view that it is more a matter of young people earning the right to belong to the group of those they admire for their courage or their defiance of the status quo. Parents are frequently blamed for allowing their children to follow radical heroes but have a great problem in that situation. They may wish to preserve the religion and culture of their origins but by no means wish to support radical and violent belief systems. They see uncertainty in Western society about religious belief. As a result, for them belief has become a precious possession under considerable threat.

Judging by Western media in the twenty-first century, there is considerable confusion about the nature of religion and the question whether we are angry about fundamentalism. We might, on the other hand be supportive of it on the grounds that it might benefit society. For example, religion might create and maintain a moral climate. In religious areas of experience, a person is presented with an immutable position. No-one can change his race or the culture into which he is born. Yet the area of religion is one where, at least in theory, there is some possibility of choice. If this were not so, there could be no possibility of conversion. People would not suddenly experience the bliss of conviction, discovering that they believe in Jesus, Mohammed or the Noble Eightfold Path.

If belief can be acquired, it can also be lost. This seems to be the case for many people. A Eurobarometer poll in 2010 on the personal religious background of Europeans established that 37% of people in the UK believe in God and 25% do not believe in any god or spiritual being. (TNS Opinion & Social 2010). A 2014 YouGov poll found that 50% of the population do not 'regard themselves as belonging to any particular religion', compared to 43% who do. It also found that only 3% of the population consider themselves to be 'very religious' and only 20% 'fairly religious', while 37% consider themselves to be 'not very religious' and 40% 'not religious at all'. (Humanists UK 2019)

Approaching religion as a choice emphasises belief in the story. Each religion has a narrative that gives its own form of comfort and reassurance. On the other hand, it is much easier to mock an account of events in Roman Judah than to come up with an alternative explanation for the foundation of the Universe in the Big Bang. Neo-atheists such as Richard Dawkins (2006) have concentrated on the beliefs in religious systems but others such as Jonathan Haidt (2012) have looked more at the social aspect of religion.

> Religions that do a better job of binding people together and suppressing selfishness spread at the expense of other religions but not necessarily by killing off the losers.
>
> (Haidt 2012: 299)

Haidt is making the point that the growth of a religion is not parallel to the development of people through genetic changes. Atran and Heinrich

(2010) have argued that there is unlikely to be any genetic connection to religiosity. They point to the rapid spread of Islam in the seventh and eighth centuries. Religions with moralistic compulsions are relatively recent in the history of mankind and there has been insufficient time for any genetic modifications to have influenced their prevalence since the beginning of cultural history.

What makes for a successful religion does of course include beliefs that answer questions such as:

- How did the world begin?
- What does death mean?

We would usually expect religious answers to include a supernatural being, but Haidt's argument is that the important phenomena are on three dimensions:

- believing,
- doing,
- belonging.

Of these three, the most significant factor in fundamentalism often is belonging. There is a variety of evidence that belonging is one of the main motives for adopting a religion and that the religion grows in strength and complexity from the number of people who are committed to it. Richard Sosis (2000) examined the life story of communes in the nineteenth century in the United States. He found that 20 years after their founding only 6% of the secular groups survived, in contrast to 39% of the religious groups. We could expect that the belief in a divine being might give comfort or provide discipline. Sosis found sacrifice and discipline to be the strongest factors, which gives some support to this view. Sharing in sacrifice and joining others in submission to discipline as in the monastic life seems to have had the capacity to bind members together.

In spite of the binding power of religion, the UK is seeing a decline in religious participation. Does this decline in religious conviction lead to a decline in moral purpose and conviction? Humanists UK is an organisation which promotes the idea that morality should be based on our belonging to humanity rather than on revealed or traditional religion. They quote a number of studies that show a continuing decline in religious belief and involvement. There are considerable regional variations. In the United States, Alabama has the highest number of people describing themselves as 'very religious' and New England States, notably New Hampshire, have the lowest with percentages in the low 30s (Lipka & Wormald 2016). If the social theory of religious belief has value, we would expect that each State would have its own religious character and that does seem to be borne out by these figures. If you have strong fundamentalist religious views you will prefer to live in a State that is full of other people with the same outlook. That will be likely to reinforce and intensify your own views.

Looking at fundamentalism among young Muslims, a social theory seems to help in understanding the impulse to go to join others. Sayeeda Warsi points out that the terrorists who bombed London in 2007 were ordinary young men from ordinary British families but they had a strong feeling of connection to their Muslim brothers in distant lands. Muslim politics has a word for this specific concept, namely 'ummah', meaning the commonwealth of the believers in Islam. The London terrorists wanted to kill people in Britain who did not seem to understand them, their religion or their feelings. Presumably the terrorists did not feel as closely connected to British communities as to Muslim ones. Warsi draws the analogy with IRA terrorists who had a stronger feeling of unity with Irish brothers who fought for union with the south of Ireland than with their geographically closer communities in the north.

Developing morality as a certainty

Teaching religion in schools has been one way of making sure that the children associate religion with a sense of belonging and beliefs with the authority of their teachers. This does not always work and many of those people who no longer believe will still have been educated in schools where religion is part of the curriculum. The requirement that was set up in 1994 for State-funded schools in the UK is for a daily act of worship with a broadly Christian approach:

> A 'broadly Christian' act of worship must contain some elements which relate to the traditions of Christian belief and which accord a special status to Jesus Christ.
>
> (Department for Education 1994: paragraph 63)

In spite of this, atheism or agnosticism is increasing in the population. We might therefore be justified in thinking that in spite of the possibility of indoctrination through what is permitted in State-funded schools, there is little enthusiasm among teachers and head teachers to produce children who are Christians. This will of course vary with individuals, and some sects of Christianity may be more evangelical than others. Schools have to teach religious education but parents can withdraw their children for all or part of the lessons. Pupils can choose to withdraw themselves once they are 18 years old. Humanists UK have paid considerable attention to the extent to which children are indoctrinated in UK schools given that, by contrast, all State education in France is required to be entirely secular. Likewise, in the United States in pursuance of the First Amendment of the

US Constitution, religious education is forbidden in public schools, except as an academic study.

If religious education is about the teaching of one religion, it will involve subscribing to a required set of beliefs. There may be no apparent indoctrination but there might still be an assumption that everyone shares the same beliefs. The adult emerging from this system will expect certainties and will often search for equivalent belief systems. In Northern Ireland communities still divide along sectarian lines, namely Protestantism and Roman Catholicism, affecting residence in city districts, politics, education, the arts, sports and festivals. Twenty years after the signing of the Good Friday Agreement that ended the euphemistically termed 'Troubles' the divisions are still, in 2020, physically manifest in some places in Belfast by actual barriers like the 40 Peace Walls totalling 30 km long. The most notorious is the wall that divides the Falls Road and Shankill Road areas in West Belfast. Communities either side of the Peace Walls demonstrate their commonality of belief with partisan murals. Displaying the wrong flags invites violent reprisals. There is a high level of certainty about what one is supposed to believe, whom one can meet and have as a friend or partner and where one goes to school or university.

In England the purpose of collective worship is supposed to be educational, intended to give pupils the opportunity to worship, or an experience of worship to evaluate or perhaps assimilate. 'Collective' worship is supposed to be different from 'corporate' worship where everyone is committed to a particular faith, as in a church, synagogue, mosque, temple or other religious setting, but it appears to be a contradiction in terms. 'Collective' is supposed to acknowledge that a school is a collection of different individuals and beliefs, and implies inclusiveness and no commitment to any particular faith. 'Worship', however, implies reverence for a divine being and thus excludes most Buddhists and Jains, and certainly excludes humanists and other non-religious pupils and teachers. Whatever schools make of the legal requirements, school children are unlikely to receive the kind of single-minded Christian belief system, mainly that of the Church of England, that was taken for granted in the 1950s and 60s. We can expect that children are increasingly less likely to have Christianity as a given from childhood than those brought up in previous years. The decline in the number of adults who say that they believe in God might indicate the extent to which religious belief relates to the environment of childhood.

If childhood experience is important in forming the religious beliefs of adults, is it the only factor that can be isolated?

Since the experience of childhood is not enough to convince the majority of the population in Britain of the existence of the Christian God, we can legitimately enquire into what sort of factors are the ones that were present in the more religious past but are less visible now. Do we now pay more attention to the rational argument and do we require a particularly high level of proof before we believe in the supernatural?

Believers would very probably assert that they have used reason and logic in order to arrive at their point of view but this tends to be after the basic premise is accepted. If the Bible is the word of God and the Koran is the same, as communicated through the words of Mohammed, then it is logical that their precepts should be obeyed. Fundamentalism may be either an expression of intellectual humility in submitting to a higher authority or intellectual pride in thinking others wrong. In both cases we have to understand the initial choice.

Underlying religious teaching there is a certainty which cannot be proved by reason and logic. Christian children are told the stories of the Bible as facts. From an early age they learn that a belief differs from a rational conclusion. It does not require evidence in the usual sense although often the holder of the belief will think that he or she has evidence. A woman who had identified as an atheist reported that while she was watching a performance of one of the York mystery plays she suddenly knew that its religious message was true. We have no way of knowing how she knew this, and still less why the story was so convincing, in spite of her former convictions.

What does religion do?

If religion is conviction underpinned by powerful emotions, defining it in a way which limits it usefully is not easy. A religion is a set of beliefs, where the word is used to denote anything from the belief in and worship of a superhuman controlling power, especially a personal God or gods to a pursuit or interest followed with great devotion.

The psychoanalyst David Black (1993) in a paper entitled 'What sort of thing is a religion?' considers the arguments that Freud put forwards in *The Future of an Illusion* (Freud 1927) in which he discusses religion's origins, development and future. Freud arrived at the conclusion that religion is wish fulfilment because it is not based on verifiable evidence. Black argues that religion is not about verifiable facts. It is a socially constructed set of internal objects or psychological realities which must be judged by different criteria from physical facts.

Black begins with Freud's view expressed mostly in his work *The Future of an Illusion* (1927). We may summarise Freud's main points very briefly.

Adult human beings, and still more 'our wretched, ignorant and downtrodden ancestors', are helpless in many situations in life. This causes them, like children, to long for a protecting father who will calm their fears, and this wish is fulfilled by the illusion of a God. Similarly, we are continually having to make painful decisions, with no certainty as

to our rightness or wisdom in doing so. A set of absolute moral com-
mandments allays our anxiety about right and wrong. Finally, our fear
and sorrow in relation to death, both our own and that of others, is
allayed by the illusion of an 'after-life' – particularly gratifying if we
can also believe that for our enemies and those we envy the after-life
will be an experience of horrible suffering. With so many advantages,
as Freud says, no wonder religion has been so successful.

(1993: 614)

Freud's attitude is negative and has led to a particularly derogatory form
of atheism. Black points out that religion serves a useful purpose for many
people and since it is not based on rational argument it cannot be refuted
by rational argument. This brings us back to the choice. Each person must
choose for himself whether the teaching of a particular religion is true and
then must hold on to his beliefs with noting to support him but passionate
intensity.

Not all religious belief is passionate or intense. Contemporary usage
attaches the name of religion to systems that have no central supernatural
figure, such as 'the religion of consumerism'. Some would consider Communism or psychoanalysis as religions. These systems would demonstrate
the importance of cohesiveness in human life and do not need gods and
mythical beings. Gods and religious beliefs are, according to Haidt (2012),
'group level adaptations to produce cohesiveness and trust ... created by
members of the group and they then organise the activity of the group'
(2012: 306).

Communism is an important system of belief with no apparent supernatural element. On the other hand, one way of looking at a religion is that it
looks to the 'superhuman'. In this sense Communism meets the definition.
Leaders of Communist States have taken on aspects of divinity and require
worship. This applies not only to the leaders of the great Communist
empires of Russian and China but also to the Dear Leader of North
Korea. The State requires sacrifice and submission and in return provides
belonging and certainties, such as the grandiosity of patriotic fervour.

Many would argue that Communism also provides passion and purpose.
Perhaps that in itself demonstrates that the most important aspect of what
constitutes a religion is that it provides certain qualities to the life of those
who subscribe to it. Psychoanalysis does the same. It has its founding
father. Freud is not quite worshipped but he did require strict orthodoxy
from his followers. Psychoanalysis provides a strong sense of belonging
and offers a way of seeing the world and other people which once acquired
is never lost. This brings us back to the three aspects named by Haidt (p.
XX) and particularly to 'belonging'.

The more exacting a religion is, the more it provides for its followers.
Rebecca Stott (2017) has written a memoire about her father and her own

life as a member of the Exclusive Brethren, a fundamentalist Christian sect in the United Kingdom and worldwide. She describes what it meant to her childhood:

> They told us that everyone outside the Brethren was Satan's army and they were all out to get us. They called them 'worldly' or 'worldlies'. If you didn't do exactly what they said they'd expel you. Then your family wouldn't be allowed to speak to you ever again. People committed suicide. People went mad.
>
> (2017:18)

What began as a wonderful sense of having the truth could become a terrifying exile. Stott describes the hope that all members of the Brethren would be gathered up into Paradise when the Rapture arrives. This is the name given by such sects to the second coming of Christ foretold in the Book of Revelation in the Bible.

An opportunity for spiritual pride

It is not enough to be a member of such a cult. You could derive satisfaction from sharing rules that separate you from the common mass of the 'Worldlies'. In the case of the Brethren, the rules were largely matters of prohibition:

> We ... weren't allowed to cut our hair. We weren't allowed television, newspapers, radios, cinemas holidays, pets, wristwatches.
>
> (Stott 2017)

Stott describes the distress that was caused when it was decided that members of the Brethren must not belong to Trades Unions or even professional societies. Many lost their jobs as a result and in many cases it led to them leaving the Brethren. For those who stayed, there was even more satisfaction to be found in sacrifice and struggle. The text that they were following was 'Come out from among them and be separate'. This was a requirement for humble submission to the rules. It was at the same time an opportunity for pride and satisfaction. It was also emphasising that being separate was being a member of a group to which you would for ever belong.

Humble submission was required, and it was not only to the word of the Bible but to the way in which the leaders of the sect interpreted it. For example, a rule was introduced in the 1960s that interpreted keeping separate as not eating with outsiders. This caused great problems at work as well as in all forms of sociability. This rule tested willingness to submit to the extent that many thought of leaving altogether, but the social implications were immense. '[When I] was thinking about leaving the fellowship altogether, a friend had written back: "Are you really prepared to kill your mother?"' (2017: 167). If Rebecca Stott had come to a therapist, she would have needed patient acceptance of the dangers of scepticism to her whole way of life and her closest relationships. Sadly, a person in that position would be most unlikely to dare to consult someone outside the Brotherhood.

Religion and morality

Religious truth cannot be established by reason. 'Credo quia absurdum' (I believe because it's absurd) was Tertullian's phrase about what is required to believe the central story of Christianity. It does not limit the number of absurdities that any individual might have to accept. Richard Dawkins (2006) has spoken about the argument that religion is valuable because it can provide an eye that watches and thus prevents us from committing the crimes that desire might lead us to commit. Although he does not think that this is an argument even for the social value of religion, never mind its truth, he is aware of research that shows greater likelihood of contributing to a collection box if a person is being watched by another person, or even if there are only pictures of eyes on the box (Bateson et al. 2013).

This is an argument that believes some convictions may be useful and lead to a better society even if they are affirming what is not true. The therapist may have trouble with the conflict of her valuing of truth with her valuing of the happiness or contentment of the patient. Carol, the trainee studying psychotherapy (Chapter 3) who was finding difficulty in accepting the members of her training group, had problems not only with Mandy but also with one man, Chris, who was a self-proclaimed Christian. He and Mel formed an alliance in which they both listened to all patients through the filter of whether they met the moral requirements that the therapists brought from their religious faith. Carol had become an atheist after a Christian upbringing. She had arrived at University with her middle of the road Anglican faith intact but there met others in the History Department who were Marxists and thought that religion was merely to keep the ordinary people happy. She had begun to believe that all educated people were atheists and was surprised to come up against Chris who had a degree in Social Science and could not be considered uneducated. To begin with she found it difficult to challenge Chris. He was authoritative and took it for granted that others would respect his views. Carol found that her old respect for the vicars of her childhood came to the fore and it seemed bad taste to bring up her reductionist views since Chris had said that he hoped that studying Freud would not involve adopting his 'discredited reductionist theories' about religion.

One of Carol's problems was that she did not know much about Freud's theories before she began the training. She knew in outline that he regarded the belief in a paternal God as an attempt at wish fulfilment in which there would be an all-giving, all-loving father. Carol hastened to get hold of *The Future of an Illusion* (Freud 1927) but felt on very shaky ground as she had not read any contemporary critiques. The whole group was inclined to receive Chris's pronouncements with respect but often also with silence or after a short pause a different point of view.

Carol found this hard to interpret until one day she found the courage to ask June to have coffee after the course. June was an older woman who was often quiet but seemed to Carol to have an intelligent and wise view of the ideas that were being discussed. She thought that June might be a friend. When they sat and talked after the next meeting, June admitted that she also had a degree but in English. 'I think they really wanted medics or at least scientists. We are letting down the academic level of the training', she said with a smile. Carol felt free to acknowledge her own doubts about her knowledge and her fear about challenging views such as those of Chris. Then it occurred to her, 'But he is a social worker not a scientist. Why is it so difficult to challenge him?' 'I think', said June,

> that it's like the teacher at school who could simply enter the room and without having to say anything was greeted with silence and order. There were others who could shout themselves hoarse but had no effect. He just has that quality but he doesn't convince people that he's right, does he? He doesn't convince me and I think not you either?

Carol was greatly relieved by this conversation and her place in the course was transformed by a growing friendship with June. She did not entirely accept June's view of the reason for the difficulty in challenging Chris. She thought about it more and went back to the danger that she found for herself in challenging religion. God had been immensely powerful to her in childhood and adolescence. Church had been connected with her mother who always took her to church. She had loved the words of the Anglican liturgy and the King James translation of the Bible. She did not want the Christian story all to be merely a myth. Freud was right, she thought, it is about wishing. I wish it was true. It is an excellent story. This led her to think about her position on other religions. She already was seeing a training patient who was a Muslim. She had to recognise that she was able to be respectful of difference and even accept the cultural requirement for the Hijab that her patient wore. Carol's supervisor agreed that it was difficult to separate the person from the culture. When she thought about the position of women, she was angry with all fundamentalist forms of religion. 'Well', said her supervisor, 'you can't do this work unless you can put your own beliefs on one side. On the other hand, you are very unlikely to see any fundamentalists in therapy. They will not want to risk it'.

Carol found this last remark very unsatisfactory. She reflected that any of her beliefs about the values of her way of life were likely to be challenged although the majority of patients were likely to belong to the liberal educated elite. She told her supervisor that she was very unhappy about this problem. This discussion led them back to the purpose of the therapist. Psychotherapist Sian Morgan, speaking at the Cambridge Festival of Ideas in 2019, said, 'I broadly believe that what brings about change in psychotherapy is careful listening, so that the patient feels truly heard, a shared humanity, genuineness, bearing witness to trauma, gentle humour and compassion'.

This sums up the main requirement that the work makes of the therapist. There is no need to believe what the patient believes but there is no need to challenge it either unless it is harming the patient. Perhaps the main purpose of a good training for a therapist should be to ensure that no harm is done and that questions are always asked.

If we believe that fundamentalism is the result of fear that beliefs are not secure enough, we have to conclude that change comes about through confidence that each individual can hold to his or her beliefs without too much risk. The very nature of the beliefs will be changed into something less violent and challenging if the holder is no longer trying to fight off those who do not agree. The experience of a therapist who is willing to disagree peaceably may be enough to enable such beliefs to moderate.

Religion is common to all societies as far as we know and speaks to a need in the human psyche for a wisdom beyond our own which is usually conceptualised as a father or male god of some sort although mother goddesses can also be found. This god is then addressed with the respect and honour which could be offered to the good father. We also know that groups revere their own gods and are likely to be jealous of the honour and respect that they guard with words and physical aggression. Anyone outside that group is likely to become the enemy. Unfortunately, therapists are all too aware that they might be seen as outside the group if they challenge religious conviction or any profoundly held belief that has been in some way related to the image of the parent who either existed or should have existed. This is one of the reasons why many therapies take a long time to work through. There has to be enough trust on both sides to take the risks.

The next chapter considers the founding faith of psychoanalysis.

References

Arditti, M. (2009) *The Enemy of the Good*. London: Arcadia Books.
Atran, S. (2014) 'Jihad's fatal attraction' *The Guardian* 4 Sep 2014.

Atran, S. & Heinrich, J. (2010) 'The evolution of religion cognitive by products, adaptive learning, heuristics, ritual displays, and group competition generate deep commitment to prosocial religions' *Biological Theory* 5: 18–30.

Bateson, M., Callow, L., Holmes, J.R., Redmond Roche, L.M., & Nettle, D. (2013) 'Do images of 'watching eyes' induce behaviour that is more pro-social or more normative? A field experiment on littering' *PLoS One* 8(12): e82055. doi:10.1371/journal.pone.0082055.

Black, D.M. (1993) 'What sort of a thing is a religion? a view from object-relations theory' *International Journal of Psychoanalysis* 74: 613–625.

Dawkins,R. (2006) *The God Delusion*. London: Bantam Press.

Department for Education. (1994) *Religious Education and Collective Worship*, Circular number 1/94.

Freud, S. (1927) *The Future of an Illusion*. S.E. 21. London: Hogarth Press.

Haidt, J. (2012) *The Righteous Mind*. London: Penguin Books.

Home Affairs Select Committee. (2012) 'Written evidence submitted by the Home Office', *The Roots of Violent Radicalisation* Nineteenth Report of Session 2010–12 Volume I, London: The Stationery Office.

Humanists UK. (2019) 'Religion and belief: some surveys and statistics' https://humanism.org.uk/campaigns/religion-and-belief-some-surveys-and-statistics/

Lipka, M. & Wormald, B. (2016) 'How religious is your state?' Fact tank website of the Pew Research Center www.pewresearch.org/fact-tank/2016/02/29/how-religious-is-your-state/

Macgrath, R. (2016) *Inclusive Masculinities in Contemporary Football: Men in the Beautiful Game*. Oxford: Taylor & Francis.

Panikkar, R. (1997) 'Nine ways not to talk about God' *Cross Currents* Summer 1997, 47(2): 1–7.

Roberts, A. (2009) *The Major Works [of Tennyson]* (ed. A. Roberts). Oxford: University Press.

Sosis, R. (2000) 'Religion and intra-group cooperation: preliminary results of a comparative analysis of utopian communities' *Cross-Cultural Research* 34: 70–87.

TNS Opinion & Social. (2010) *Eurobarometer 73.1: Biotechnology*. Brussels: TNS Opinion & Social.

Warsi, S. (2017) *The Enemy Within*. London: Penguin Books.

Winnicott, D.W. (1974) 'Transitional objects and transitional phenomena' in *Playing and Reality* (pp. 1–30). London: Pelican Books.

Chapter 5

Certainty in theory

What I want is men who will support me when I am in the wrong.
William Lamb, Lord Melbourne

Lord Melbourne was Prime Minister in the mid-nineteenth century. His ironic tone expresses the truth for most politicians, who survive on supporting votes. Everyone wishes her theory to be supported but not all would say that they wanted to be supported if they were wrong. This chapter will consider the way in which writers and thinkers convey their openness to changing or modifying their convictions. Freud is an example of someone who has been much accused of being wrong. However, as well as being passionately committed to the ideas of psychoanalysis, he was in fact a writer who could be open to reconsidering the validity of his own statements.

Freud was undoubtedly capable of real anger when challenged. His quarrels with Carl Jung and other of his followers and friends such as Josef Breuer and Wilhelm Fliess show this. The distinction seems to be that he could accept that he had changed his mind, as he did over his theory of sexual seduction. However, he could not bear to lose the unquestioning admiration of such followers as Jung, Breuer and Fliess. This chapter will draw on Freud's controversial statements about sexuality followed by his work on the Oedipus complex.

According to the poet, W. H. Auden (1940) by the mid-twentieth century Freud had become a 'whole climate of opinion'. Freud's emphasis on the unconscious and the prevalence of sexuality in mental life had made his climate of opinion very difficult to accept, but by the time Auden was writing there was already an orthodoxy. Most of Freud's difficulties centred on his proposition that all neurotic illness arises from the sexual abuse of young children. His later great theoretical proposition was his account of the Oedipus complex in which the young child harbours wishes to have the love of the opposite sex parent and wishes to get rid of the rival, the same sex parent. Freud initially acquired fanatical followers to promote and defend his attitudes and points of view. On the other hand, he was vehemently opposed by those who found this kind of delving into what they did not and could not control too alarming to tolerate. Anyone who has been involved with any of the main training schools in psychoanalysis will be aware of the vehemence and often the bitterness of the disputes that have developed. Freud is not blameless in these disputes. His own desire for both fame and unquestioning allegiance was intense.

Since it evokes such passions, some have called psychoanalysis a religion. For most people, to call it a religion is to criticise the passionate conviction of its devotees and to ignore the moderate views of those who think that it can be helpful although not the answer to everything. There can be little doubt that psychoanalysis is in some ways in the position of being a religion. It has accumulated believers. Because many have devoted their lives to promoting one model of the human mind, they cannot easily allow another point of view that might be equally valid.

In the first edition (1895) of the work by Freud and his collaborator Josef Breuer on hysteria, Freud wrote in the preface in a way that set a tone in which controversy, or at least difference of opinion between them could initially be tolerated:

> If at some points, divergent and indeed contradictory opinions are expressed, this is not to be regarded as any fluctuation in our views. It arises from the justifiable differences between the opinions of two observers ... but who are not invariably at one in their interpretations and conjectures.
>
> (Freud & Breuer 1895: 48)

In the preface to the second edition (1918), Freud expresses his willingness to change his mind if the evidence points in a different direction from the one in which he was first going:

> The development and changes in my views throughout thirteen years of work have not been too far reaching ... Nor have I any reason for wishing to eliminate the evidence of my initial views. Even today I regard them not as errors but as valuable first approximations to knowledge which could only be acquired after long and continuous efforts.
>
> (Freud & Breuer 1918: 49)

This is an important principle. Freud was, however, willing to tolerate the development of his theory in his own mind but was not willing to accept divergence from his followers. The reason is perhaps that disagreement from others could not be controlled or amended. His own views could be dammed up at an acceptable point before they rushed over sweeping away too much.

Undoubtedly both Freud and Breuer had to tolerate some negative, even hostile attacks from the medical profession, as well as from the laity. In *The Aetiology of Hysteria* (Freud & Breuer 1896), they put forwards the view that hysterical neurosis had its roots in the sexual experience of the young child, which had been repressed because it was painful and unpleasurable. It took some courage to promote this theory. It cost Freud dearly in terms of his reputation as a serious physician: he needed respectable Viennese husbands to permit their wives to attend his private practice. Perhaps the difficulty of asserting and holding to this theory made Freud even more angry when those close to him cast doubts on it.

Josef Breuer was the first collaborator to suffer from disagreement with Freud. He was a distinguished doctor and neuroscientist, 14 years older than Freud. He took on the young Freud as his protégé. Breuer had helped Freud to set up his practice, giving him a considerable amount of money in a stipend which Breuer did not expect Freud to repay.

In 1882, Breuer discussed with Freud the case of the patient Bertha Pappenheim, whom they called Anna O. Freud was intrigued by the method Breuer had used and began using it with those whom he treated. Pappenheim was suffering from a severe cough, paralysis of the extremities on the right side of her body, and disturbances of vision, hearing and speech, as well as hallucinations and occasional loss of consciousness. She was diagnosed with hysteria. Initially Breuer was using hypnosis but she found that she gained more from talking to him and saying whatever came into her mind. In this way, Breuer was able to discover the benefits of free association as a method of discovering deep-seated problems from the past.

Breuer and Freud collaborated to publish a report of a lecture they had given on what Breuer was already calling the 'cathartic method' (*On the Psychical Mechanisms of Hysterical Phenomena*, Breuer & Freud 1893). Two years later, Breuer and Freud (1895) collaborated on the book *Studies on Hysteria*. It would become a foundation text for the practice of psychoanalysis. However, this publication marked the end of their friendship and collaboration as Breuer was unwilling to accept Freud's theory of the primacy of sexual abuse over other kinds of trauma in the aetiology of hysteria. Freud was angry enough to discredit Breuer. He even wrote to Stefan Zweig much later in 1932 (Gay 1988: 67) that Breuer had discontinued the treatment of Pappenheim and rushed back to his wife in a panic because Pappenheim had fallen in love with him and spoke of bearing his child. Research has since shown that the child that Breuer conceived with his wife was in fact conceived before the end of Pappenheim's treatment. In other words, Breuer was not frightened away but continued his interest in her as long as she was ill. Peter Gay points out that Freud remained in debt to Breuer financially and some of his anger may relate to the difficulty of accepting that. Most difficult for Freud was Breuer's refusal to support him in his theory. Freud wrote to Fliess in 1895:

> Breuer gave a big speech about me to the Vienna Society of physicians and introduced himself as a converted adherent to the sexual etiology of the neuroses. When I thanked him for this in private, he destroyed my pleasure by saying 'I don't believe it, all the same'.
>
> (Gay 1988: 68)

Freud was clearly hurt by this. More importantly he seems to have needed the support of his former mentor to help him to remain convinced of the value of his sexual theory of childhood seduction even in the face of ridicule and criticism. Without such support and without his own conviction he had to think again and that was likely to be unwelcome.

Wilhelm Fliess is another man with whom Freud eventually ended what had been a very important relationship. Again, it was the lack of support for a concept that Freud himself found difficult to believe that was at least in part responsible for the rupture. In his relationship and correspondence with Fliess he found, in the same person, both a dear friend and, later, an enemy. From their first acquaintance in 1887, to their estrangement which Freud acknowledged in 1901, Fliess played the role of confidant and understanding male listener, perhaps the nearest Freud was able to find to an analyst of his own. On the other hand, Freud had lost his own younger brother, Julius, in 1858 at less than a year old and was perhaps looking for a vigorous and lively sibling. By the time Freud was ready to publish *The Interpretation of Dreams* in 1900, he was able to see that Fliess's own convictions concerning mysticism and superstitions, such as the value of numerology, were ideas that he could not accept. They attacked each other's convictions when they met in August 1900 and quarrelled in a way that could never be mended. Even so, Freud was still grateful to Fliess, recognising that Fliess had contributed to Freud's ability to develop his ideas.

Conviction without flexibility or tolerance is demonstrated in the sad end to several of Freud's friendships. The most well-known break was the end of his connection with the Swiss psychologist, Carl Jung. In 1907, when they met, Freud, a Jew, was 51 and Jung, a Protestant, was 37. The age difference alone would lead us to think of transference for each of them of father and son. Each wanted the good will, even love, of the other — for different reasons. Jung's friendship and Christianity were important to Freud: together, they helped him be accepted by the dominant class in Vienna. The story is well known, but the reasons for their estrangement seem to relate at least in part to Freud's difficulty in allowing his transferential son to grow into a potential rival and to Jung's difficulty in being repressed by a powerful but needy father; unintentionally, Freud was confirming his own Oedipal theory. The context is also important. Freud was

suffering attacks from other doctors over his seduction theory. In spite of
the distress that the split between them caused, each one strengthened their
own position and developed very different but equally fruitful approaches
to understanding the human psyche.

Changing his mind

Freud felt that he had certainly suffered a great deal at the hands of the
medical establishment in Vienna after his first lecture on the origins of hysteria in sexual seduction in April 1896. Frank Sulloway (1992: 82) shows
that there were favourable reviews and responses from such writers as
Pierre Janet and Eugen Bleuler. Sulloway believes that Freud can be seen
sometimes to seek to isolate himself because he wanted to see himself as
the solitary hero. 'Freud never stopped feeling isolated no matter how
famous he later became. He continued to act like a man who daily faced
the dangerous fire of the enemy' (1992: 478).

Whatever Freud's unconscious motivation for feeling persecuted might
have been, he did face some negative views. For example, Richard Krafft-
Ebing (1896) expressed doubt that a talking cure could effectively cure hysteria. Since Freud himself had begun to doubt the validity of his own
theory that sexuality was the basis of all hysterical reactions, he had to
regard himself as a lone and courageous hero, identified perhaps with
Moses (Sulloway 1992: 477).

However much importance this hero archetype had for him, Freud had
the intellectual integrity to acknowledge that the evidence did not always
support his statements. In his first great disavowal of previous conviction,
some of his detractors have even accused Freud of giving in to attacks,
making this reaction and therefore self-interest the whole reason for his
change of mind. This position was emphasised by Jeffery Masson (1992)
but has been refuted by writers such as Alan Esterson (2001). Since then,
much argument and controversy has arisen over the reasons for the abandonment of the universal sexual trauma theory. In 1897 he confessed to
Fliess that he had to reconsider his theory of the part played by sexual
seduction in infants, a theory for which he coined the term 'Neurotica'. In
his letters, he gave three reasons for doubting the reality of these seductions and beginning to think that they were fantasies, or even wishes,
rather than something that had actually happened (Masson 1985). In
a letter of September 23 1897, he confided to Fliess: 'I no longer believe in
my Neurotica'.

Freud had to assess the validity of the stories of sexual abuse being told
him by some female patients, but most of all he had to be honest with
himself. He had just embarked on his self-analysis in which he made what
was indeed a heroic attempt to be honest and to hold his conscious certainties up to the light. In the preface to his monumental work, *The*

Interpretation of Dreams (Freud 1900), which he considered to arise in part from self-analysis, he points out that he has used his own dreams and therefore exposed himself to the public gaze in a way that is usually more characteristic of poets.

In the matter of theory Freud had been faced with great disappointment and uncertainty. He could not at that time claim the great scientific advance that he had hoped for, since he had rejected the sexual theory of the origin of all neurosis. His self-analysis however led him towards a recognition of the importance of the Oedipus complex. He saw that among all the chaos of images and thoughts in dreams there was much evidence of the importance of the mothers, fathers, brothers and sisters of human beings, not just neurotic patients themselves.

Although the disavowal letter to Fliess might imply a clinical reason for rejecting the theory that all neurosis is caused by infantile sexual abuse, Freud adduces three other arguments. The most well known is that he was willing to reconsider his position because it involved blaming all fathers including his own. At this point he became very disturbed by the conclusions that he was drawing from his self-analysis. If he considered seduction a universal event, then he had to accuse his own father of carrying out the same practice. Secondly, he could not accept that the same cause would be valid for all children. He had seen that children grew into very different adults with different neuroses and he argued that children had individual early experiences. Finally, the unconscious does not distinguish truth from falsehood and therefore the analyst cannot be sure whether he is hearing about an experience that happened or a wish for an experience that should have happened. He expected that, if these infantile seductions were being repressed, memories would have emerged in some form; but in his experience no such consistent memories had emerged, even under hypnosis. He wrote to Fliess in 1897:

> I was so far influenced [by this] that I was ready to give up two things: the complete resolution of a neurosis and the certain knowledge of its aetiology in childhood. Now I have no idea of where I stand because I have not succeeded in gaining a theoretical understanding of repression and its interplay of forces. It seems once again arguable that only later experiences give the impetus to fantasies, which [then] hark back to childhood, and with this the factor of a hereditary disposition regains a sphere of influence from which I had made it my task to dislodge it – in the interest of illuminating neurosis.
>
> (Masson 1985, letter of Sept 21 1897)

In 1895 Freud already had doubts about his theory of repression. If childhood sexual experiences lead to repression and repression leads to adult symptoms such as hysteria or obsessionality, how do we account for different outcomes in different people?

Frank Sulloway (1992) discusses the way in which Freud developed and changed his thinking about this fundamental strand of theory for psychoanalysis. If all infantile abuse is painful and leads to guilt, the theory of repression makes sense. There was a troubling paradox. Since much of Freud's theoretical structure rests upon the pleasure found in sexuality, why would we see repression of the memories of what had been pleasurable? Guilt could be seen to cause this repression but why would there not always have been a compulsive need to repeat any sexual experiences that were pleasurable? In fact, we do see this in some adults who have been abused as children but not universally as the theory would require.

Freud had to recognise that there were problems in his theoretical positions. Considering that they were leading to severe reactions from the medical and psychiatric community that might deprive him of patients and thence of an income to support his wife and growing family, he had to be very careful. In a letter to Fliess on 30 June 1896 he even asked Fliess to help him by suggesting an explanation that would depend on physiology – so giving it a firm footing and of course it would then be less subject to scorn and dislike from his fellow doctors.

This is a change of mind from a position that Freud had originally defended with courage and conviction. Of course, it had far-reaching effects in the theory and practice of psychoanalysis. It has led to the present-day emphasis on attempts to understand the way in which wishes subvert the experience of reality in talking therapies.

Blind adherence

The myth of Oedipus tells us that he blinded himself as a way of responding to the guilt of what he had seen and done. This is an image that conveys much of the reaction that we find when people are confronted with a painful or shocking truth. Freud told Fliess about a dream in 1897 soon after his father's death had left him with the powerful phrase 'close the eyes'.

> I must tell you about a nice dream I had the night after the funeral. I was in a place where I read a sign: You are requested to close the eyes. I immediately recognized the location as the barbershop I visit every day. On the day of the funeral I was kept waiting and therefore arrived a little late at the house of mourning. At that time my family was displeased with me because I had arranged for the funeral to be quiet and simple, which they later agreed was quite justified. They were also somewhat offended by my lateness. The sentence on the sign has a double meaning: one should do one's duty to the dead (an

apology as though I had not done it and were in need of leniency), and the actual duty itself. The dream thus stems from the inclination to self-reproach that regularly sets in among the survivors.

(Masson 1985: 202)

This can be understood as either an instruction to give his father peace or it can be something more about not letting him see. Blindness is connected with the father who needs the eyes to be closed. Much of the work that is done in psychoanalysis is an effort to uncover the truth of a person's mental process and to show him the kind of self-deception that he is practising.

Perhaps there is a clue here as to the difficulty of changing one's mind. There is at least a hint that Freud saw the possibility that the injunction to close the eyes was to close his own eyes and referred to his own perceptions. There is a risk to the father also if he can see too much, in having the son's eyes open when his father might be fallible or weak. In this area of betraying the parents or surpassing the father lies a problem we all have in moving away from childhood to adulthood. Not all analysts, psychotherapists or counsellors are willing to see the dangers of self-deception in themselves and even those who pay lip service to this danger find it as difficult as anyone else to face the truth and make changes accordingly.

Freud was always interested in deception, particularly self-deception. The myth of Oedipus spoke to the matter of self-deception. An oracle foretells that Laius, King of Thebes, will be killed by his own son, who will then marry his mother. In order to avoid this fate, Laius and his wife Jocasta cause their son, Oedipus, to be abandoned on a hillside where he is adopted by a shepherd and his wife, Polybus and Merope. Oedipus himself is told about the oracle's prophecy and mistakes its meaning, thinking that it means that he will kill his foster parents. He leaves them and sets off for Thebes, where he kills Laius and marries Jocasta: the prediction of the oracle comes true.

Freud tried to balance this kind of determinism with his belief in the power of the ego to change by thinking, but for him the unconscious had something of the force of a decree of the fates in Greek mythology. The myth shows that the ego is not able to defy the wishes of the unconscious. The story ends with blinding; Oedipus blinds himself in reaction to discovering what he had done. Freud developed this idea when writing of his dream just after his father's death. He knew that guilt and self-reproach accompany mourning but that they in turn are hidden.

Certainty in the training institutes

Freud's dream also included the reproaches of relatives who are not happy that the dreamer had arrived late at the funeral. The individual lives within a social context. There is no malice in the story of Oedipus except from the gods, but there is certainly suffering and guilt in human experience. Not surprisingly, psychoanalysis itself gives us illustrations of disputes in which the participants have held passionate and firmly entrenched beliefs which have led to fierce, ad hominem arguments. These disputes often have an oedipal edge to them. One of the best known of these was the disagreement between Anna, Freud's daughter, and Melanie Klein. These disputes were not just a matter of two powerful women defending their positions, although they were certainly that. The disputes were in fact about fundamental questions of the nature of transference and the technique that followed from it. Klein used her play technique with children, which Anna Freud denounced as a departure from the classical tradition left to us by Freud. For his daughter Freud's word was law. It could not be questioned, let alone found to be wrong. The American analyst Dr Arthur Couch came to train in London in 1967 having begun his training in Boston and was shocked at the level of conviction and passionate certainty that he found in London. He greatly admired Anna Freud whom he took as his training analyst but the level of support for Klein in London surprised him. He found that many senior analysts there

> conveyed that they were part of a separate tradition of analysis that began in London, founded by Jones, Strachey, Melanie Klein and Winnicott – and now continued by Bion, Rosenfeld, Segal, Balint and Khan. Freud was revered, but it seemed his 'old' ideas had been supplanted by new English theories. In my early years here, I kept shaking my head. How could these people have been converted so completely to these new theories and have disregarded the major contributions of the past several decades of Viennese analysts who emigrated to America plus Anna Freud who stayed in London and many eminent American analysts? After twenty-five years I still shake my head at this insular development.
>
> (Sinasson 1995: 367)

Anna Freud's certainty derived in part from the fact the Freud was her father whom she greatly respected and protected fiercely after his death. She had also been analysed by him. Both of these sorts of loyalty can be immensely powerful in convincing people that they must defend and protect some aspect of a parent, especially when the parent is dead or out of reach in the way that an analyst who is no longer being seen is felt to be. This might lead to the hypothesis that the defence and protection of the dead father is felt to be needed as a way of keeping him alive.

The opposite case can be seen with Melitta Shmideberg who did all in her power to kill off her mother Melanie Klein, at the metaphorical level, in the papers in which Schmideberg demonstrated her loyalty to Freud.

One possible cause of her hostility was the death of her brother in a climbing incident, which she thought was suicide and for which she blamed her mother. Melanie Klein was no doubt a difficult mother, one whom a daughter could easily be led to challenge partly because there was no way of arguing with her:

> Her claims were becoming increasingly extravagant, she demanded unquestioning loyalty and tolerated no disagreement.
>
> (Grosskurth 1986: 216)

We can see there in practice the power of the oedipal position. Klein's daughter demonstrated the degree of rivalry with the mother, which can lead to positions that are damaging to the relationship and may never be healed.

> Like Freud, Klein demanded undivided loyalty. Like Freud she could be ruthless in casting off those who expressed doubts.
>
> (Grosskurth 1986: 216)

In the split between them, Anna Freud defended her father and Melanie Klein's ideas diverged from Freud's. No doubt there were also personal resonances for many at the London Institute of Psychoanalysis; they could not avoid taking a position that was determined by who was their own father or mother analyst.

What is very important to note in this ongoing divergence of opinion is that even though the dispute was internecine at the time, dividing the analytic world in England and beyond, the followers of each leader managed to reach a way of living together. Neither side abandoned its position. Anyone who has experienced the extreme Kleinian position will know that it is a very specific way of looking at the mind or 'the inner world'. Nevertheless, the Freudians and later the Lacanians learned to live with colleagues who in all sincerity held greatly different positions. On the other hand, both these theoretical approaches (Anna Freud's and Melanie Klein's) have made valuable contributions to the treatment of children and of adults.

Although I have chosen to focus on the British disputes, Jacques Lacan in France was also someone who would demand total adherence to his beliefs. Bela Grunberger and Janine Chasseguet-Smirgel were two psychoanalysts from the Paris section of the International Psychoanalytical Association (IPA). They published a book under a pseudonym interpreting the behaviour of the students rebelling in Paris in 1968 as displaying an Oedipal rebellion against the paternal authorities. Lacan did not like it and said that he was certain that neither author belonged to his school, as none would abase themselves to such low drivel (Lacan 1968: 266). The IPA analysts responded with an accusation against Lacan's school of 'intellectual terrorism'.

Lacan appears to have become every bit as dogmatic as Freud and within his École Freudienne de Paris, which he founded in 1964, objection and argument were often stifled. Stories, victories and defeats all took place within those years and no brief summary can do justice to the importance of the École Freudienne in European thinking. Lacan had become a powerful personality. He advocated revolutionary thinking such as, for example his proposals that sessions could be of variable length and that a candidate might authorise himself to pass and become an analyst. At the same time, Lacan demanded adherence to what was becoming a new orthodoxy. Even in returning to Freud he superseded him. Trapped between the two opposite approaches, he dissolved his school in 1980, before it could be changed by others. The next year, he established a replacement, the École de la Cause Freudienne. It continues to teach and promote psychoanalysis. Like Freud, Lacan has come to represent a whole climate of opinion and a new orthodoxy.

Compromise

What enables an individual to compromise? In compromising, the two sides of an argument must both be allowed to have some value even if the individual cannot see what the value of the other side is and would like to wipe it out as the opposing point of view. Psychoanalytic theory would immediately suggest that here an individual needs to be able to allow both parents to have equal value. Since this is usually too much to ask and one parent is inevitably favoured over the other, the person who can make successful compromises is likely to be the one who can see beyond his own preference and allow the parent of the same sex to survive. In the case of the British Institute of Psychoanalysis, two groups of Freudians and Kleinians exist without threat; but there was also the birth of the new group who are known as the Independents. This implies that an individual who can allow co-existence can also overcome his envy enough to allow the birth of something new. In terms of the family metaphor, a new sibling to any given individual therapist might be accepted without threatening disaster.

This line of reasoning leads to the conclusion that in order to help an individual to be less fixed and opposed to change, the therapist must work on the extent to which his envy prevents him from allowing love and forgiveness to the other members of his family. To use a Kleinian view of the work that needs to be done, the position that the patient takes up becomes more flexible, more often in the depressive position, which means being more able to move round the family group, honouring and admiring each one at times and also hating each one at times but not fixedly addressing one person with only one kind of emotion.

Unconscious causes

Psychoanalysis has much to say about the structure of certainty within the mind. Freud was also very interested in the structural reasons for a high level of conviction. To understand this part of his thinking, we need to consider the theory of the unconscious that developed from *The Interpretation of Dreams* and his clinical work towards the paper of 1915 in which he set out his thinking on how our conscious certainties are subverted by the work of the 'it'. The only escape from the dangers of this position is to find words for what goes on there. What can be put into words can be thought about and then choices open up. (Freud 1915: 147).

This part of the theory of the unconscious indicates to us that the work of analytic therapy is to put words to unconscious ideas so that they can be considered and perhaps changed. In other words, the crucial process in bringing about flexibility and possible change is the process of catching the unthought ideas that are indicated in dreams, jokes, slips of the tongue and all the emotional landscape of transference in order to express these ideas in words.

This may be the ultimate aim of psychoanalysis but the only way of assessing how useful it is must be by measuring and comparing outcomes. As Peter Fonagy and Mary Target pointed out, this has proved very difficult to achieve even within one model such as psychoanalysis (Fonagy & Target 2005). Attempts to assess the outcomes of early analytic work were not encouraging. Many writers have attacked Freud on this very area. For example, Anna O was not cured of her difficulties as Freud and Breuer claimed. In fact, she may have been suffering from temporal lobe epilepsy rather than a purely psychological problem (Webster 1996). Yet she herself said that her sessions helped her. No doubt this help could be seen as transferential in that her father had recently died: Breuer was taking her seriously and providing a warm fatherly presence. Psychological therapists may have to content themselves with knowing only that their patients may be better off with the work than without it but an absolute measure of benefit is unlikely to be found.

Moving on

Freud was greatly troubled by a number of aspects of his seduction theory and outcomes were only one part of it. Most people are aware of his change from the belief that every child suffers from sexual abuse during infancy to a position in which he believed that most children only harbour wishes to be the partner of the opposite sex parent. In other words there might be unconscious sexual desire for a parent but for most people this was not about adult action. He arrived at this view partly by listening carefully to his patients and being willing to be honest about what he found. Giving up this theory, which he had defended passionately at the cost of the relationship with some of his closest friends, cost him even more dearly perhaps than espousing it in the first place. Nevertheless, once he had decided that it could not be true, he wrote to Fliess in 1897 and asked him not to speak of it yet to anyone else, telling him of the chasm that had opened up in front of him. This level of shame can accompany changing one's mind and may account for the reluctance that we encounter.

Although he saw himself as a scientist, definitely not a poet, Freud went through some depression or low mood, and what he called a 'little hysteria'. He had his dark night of the soul in which he feared for his theory and for the future of psychoanalysis. He was disappointed but as he worked on his self-analysis other aspects of human experience such as the Oedipus complex began to rescue him. First, he had to be completely honest with himself, which he knew was not easy. Looking at his own dreams and memories he found that he had desired his mother and wanted to supplant his father.

The shape of the Oedipus complex gradually formed in his mind and compensated for the earlier failure to find the root of all neurosis. This time he was able to claim that all human beings would have the same experience. This of course has been questioned by ethnologists and sociologists who take very literally the idea of the child's sexuality and love for the parent. They ask whether this phenomenon can apply in other cultures where there is often not a mother and father present. They ask about homosexual couples bringing up children. Freud however was pleased to find evidence for his theory in the analysis of the five-year-old child whom he called 'Little Hans'. From 1906 to 1908 Freud corresponded with the child's father and advised him on how to talk to his son. In this process, Freud was able to see the effects of the love for the mother and the rivalry with the father played out in detail in the father's account of his child's disturbance. Although the tone of the analyst that he adopted in writing to Hans' father in 1906 is clear and confident he no longer sounds as dogmatic as in his earlier days. Yet carrying out analysis second hand inevitably meant that he used such statements as 'I suggested' or 'his father was to say' (Masson 1985: 191).

In all the case histories, Freud shows his ability to write perceptively about the individual and not lose sight of his or her uniqueness while still being able to deduce some general principles of human behaviour. During 1897 to 1898 he wrote to Fliess about the 'family romance' and in bursts of insight began to see the theory with which he could understand a great deal of both infantile and adult behaviour. In order to make use of the Oedipal strand of his thinking he needed the work he was beginning to put together on the unconscious: 'We shall defend the complications of our theory so long as we find that they meet the results of observation' (Freud 1915: 190). In his paper on 'The Unconscious' written in 1915, Freud was willing to set out a process in which he moved from ideas that he could no longer support to a better formulation:

> The two are not as we supposed different registrations of the same content in different psychical localities ... but the conscious presentation of the thing plus the word belonging to it while the unconscious presentation is the presentation of the thing alone.
>
> (Freud 1915: 201)

He ends this paper by starting a sentence: 'If we have made a true assessment of the nature of the unconscious ...' (ibid: 204). The use of the word 'if' is significant. Freud is willing to doubt or at least to appear to doubt.

> That is by no means easy. Being totally honest with oneself is a good exercise. A single idea of general value dawned on me. I have found, in my own case too, [the phenomenon of] being in love with my mother and jealous of my father, and I now consider it a universal event in early childhood, even if not so early as in children who have been made hysterical. (Similar to the invention of parentage [family romance] in paranoia–heroes, founders of religion). If this is so, we can understand the gripping power of Oedipus Rex.
>
> (Masson 1985: letter of Oct. 15, 1897)

Oedipal theory illuminates Jeffrey Masson's autobiographical account of his own analysis. In *Final Analysis* (1990), he describes his training in Toronto and arrival in London. Instead of loving his analyst in the place of his father, he was unable to win his analyst's love and seems to have hated and resented him. Much of Masson's account is about certainty and some of its ill effects. He attacked Freud's views, and was himself attacked by the psychoanalytic establishment over his passionate statements. The book was dismissed by some critics as mere gossip. Masson's efforts to discover the truth of Freud's views on seduction were seen by most of his contemporaries as a betrayal of psychoanalysis, partly because at the same time he was 'gossiping' about the foibles of his own analyst. One of his main complaints is of the extreme self-confidence (as he portrays it) of his analyst, who seems to be saying 'I had to put up with this sort of thing and now you have to'. Without entering into any of the detail filtered through Masson's own pathology, which as for most of us includes some envy, we can see that it was the unassailable certainty of being right that he saw in his analyst that gave him so much anger and hurt.

Confirmation bias

A very short time after arriving at his new ideas about what he hoped might be universal, Freud analytically 'uncovered' the evidence to confirm it, demonstrating that his analytic technique of interpretation and reconstruction enabled him to 'corroborate' whatever theory he currently held. In other words, a very short time after arriving at an early formulation of his new theory Freud analytically 'uncovered' the evidence to confirm it. This seems a reasonable procedure. A hypothesis is developed and evidence either supports or refutes it. Conviction needs to follow this procedure but in ordinary life this is rarely the case. Opposing evidence is discounted or given little weight.

Why would a person believe that he or she is right?

Susan is a patient who has been attending psychotherapy for five years. She has a background of a neglectful mother who seemed to favour her older sister. Susan is the middle of three children. She works as an administrator and lives with a partner, Andy, whom she describes as feckless, just spending her money and not contributing. Her therapist, my supervisee, describes feelings of anger and frustration with Susan when she goes through a litany of complaints about Andy because she feels she has to do all the work. In spite of this she has left a series of jobs, always citing a boss who does not appreciate her and colleagues who talk about her behind her back or make her feel unwelcome. Her therapist thinks that all this is a repetition of her family situation where she keeps thinking that the next job will provide her with the love and appreciation that she feels she never had.

Her therapist describes a session after a break. Susan has just started a new job and she speaks angrily about how difficult the new line manager is and how angry she is with the therapist who is not helping her. The therapist has problems because she finds that whatever she tentatively puts forwards as empathy or understanding is angrily rejected while Susan goes on with her circular complaints. The supervisee says she is tired of trying to make any headway through this whirlpool of complaint and tells Susan that she does not see why anyone would hold on to her own opinion of what other people are doing to her when it seems to be so painful. This throws a stone into the water and sets up ripples of meaning for Susan to consider. As for the surface of the water, ripples disturb the smooth conviction.

Paul Hoggett (2018) has written a paper on the reasons why people hold on to complaints. Presumably one part of the value of a complaint is that it is an assertion that one is right. The emotional force of having been wronged, which is essential to a complaint, adds to the satisfaction to be gained. Asking why this provides satisfaction that is preferable to letting it go is sometimes the first step to a change.

Confirmation bias is a phenomenon that is observable in everyday life and has itself also been confirmed by psychologists in experiments. For example, Wason (1960) in the United States presented to subjects the start of a simple series of numbers: 2, 4, 6. He told them there was a rule for continuing the series and asked them to discover the rule by questioning. All subjects came up immediately with 8, 10, 12 as a proposal with its attendant rule of adding 2. They were told that it was not the rule and so they pursued other possibilities (10, 16, 26 and others). They were always unable to discover the rule in Wason's mind. It turned out to be that *any* ascending series of numbers was acceptable and the rule was much simpler than they expected. People were good at developing complex hypotheses about the way the series increased but did not make the simple test of offering a descending series. This would have shown them that this was the only kind of sequence that did not obey the rule. Wason concluded that we cherish our initial solution or belief so much that we do not even think of ideas that might bring it into question. We might be able to improve government projects like the Prevent strategy to prevent radicalization if we understand the strength of opinions once embraced. We must take into account the importance of challenging beliefs but even more the value for each individual of holding on to them.

Socially constructed truth

Truth is a large and dangerous concept. What is truth and how do we establish it? Much depends on the therapist's ideas about truth. Common answers may focus on scientific method and observation but, since Freud has taught us to take account of the subversive power of the unconscious which determines both what we perceive and how we perceive it, we have to recognise that perceptions may not lead us to truth. What any individual considers to be the way to the truth is of vital importance in any therapeutic work and will show the basis of unreasonable conviction. Only if a workable version of truth can be reached will a person be able to live in a shared universe with others. A relevant approach to truth is to see it as a socially constructed phenomenon. We seek to believe what everyone else in our group believes.

Susan perhaps approaches truth from this perspective. We can see that in an age in which women have vociferously complained about male harassment, she joins in with a social construct of the truth in terms of male power being used to subdue and control women. She has constructed a narrative in which she is the victim of powerful men who ignore her needs and her complaints. This narrative is self-consistent but seems unfortunately to be locked inside itself. There is no way for the outside world and therefore correspondence to shared reality to have any impact. One task for the therapist might be to prize open such a narrative so that some form of correspondence within the social climate is brought to bear.

When looking at Freud's level of certainty we were able to show that he wished to be seen to make propositions that were self-consistent and in accordance with observation. He certainly was not able to take the beliefs of a group such as the contemporary medical profession to be his touchstone. As his therapies gained circulation and even notoriety, he acquired strong and faithful supporters and a group coherence developed. Jeffrey Masson (1992) in his training in Canada came up against a very well-established social construction in which there could be no questioning or doubt at all. He is a writer who can tell a story well and he takes the reader with him into the experience of a trainee or candidate psychoanalyst in his day. His own analyst is described with some comic sense although anyone from the field would be more horrified than amused and therefore might be inclined to disbelief. Given that his description of the analysis is anywhere near true, he was being socialised into a position intended to lead to new analysts who would demand the same rigid adherence to the power of the role as they had experienced themselves.

The function of rigidity in training is to ensure a particular approach to moral and theoretical choices. This means moving the area of rational decision further towards the area of moral choice. Jonathan Haidt summarises the process of moral decision making:

> The first principle of moral psychology is Intuition comes first, strategic reasoning second.
> Social and political judgments depend heavily on quick intuitive flashes.
> Our bodily states sometimes influence our moral judgments.
>
> (Haidt 2012: 82)

Haidt goes on to consider the ways in which human brains are wired to find supporting evidence for the conclusion that has already been reached. Freud helps us to understand the basis on which the instantaneous judgments are reached in the first place. They are based on the confusion induced by unconscious wishes seeking to avoid the censorship of an unconscious area of the ego. Once a position has been taken in external reality, the confirmation bias to which we are all subject begins to work. Haidt points out that Plato in his *Republic* asked Socrates to prove that just or true decisions are more valuable to the individual than the appearance or reputation for truth (2012: 85). The need for man as a tribal animal to be in good standing with fellow animals is still important in spite of the argument that Plato brings forwards that the individual, like a State, benefits from an ethos of justice and truth. The lack of concern for truth and integrity seen in some political leaders in the twenty-first century might lead us to doubt this maxim, at least in the short term.

Philip Tetlock (2002) in the US carried out research that illuminates even further the extent to which social approval affects the kind of decision-making process that we are willing to use. He shows that accountability is an important feature of decision making and that the process of accounting for choices will enter into the judgments that are made Haidt's premise is that we are much more concerned with creating the appearance of virtue than with the reality which would involve a love of truth whatever the cost of that might be. 'Our moral thinking is much more like a politician searching for votes than a scientist searching for truth' (2012: 89).

This conclusion is a logical consequence of Freud's thinking that all our conscious beliefs are undermined by the power of the unconscious, which forms an unseen subversive. If the subversion from the unconscious is, as Freud thought, in the service of instinctual impulses towards sexual satisfaction, then the wish for social approval and praise is likely to be always in conflict with those wishes and will lead to the need for a strong determination to convince not only the audience but one's self. This will bring us back to the conclusion that with so much at stake, changing one's mind is profoundly difficult.

References

Auden, W.H. (1940) 'In memory of Sigmund Freud' in Auden, W.H. (Ed.), *From Another Time*. New York: Random House.

Breuer, J. & Freud, S. (1893) 'On the psychical mechanism of hysterical phenomena' in *Studies on Hysteria*, Pelican Freud library, Vol. 3 (pp. 53–72). Harmondsworth: Penguin Books.

Breuer, J. & Freud, S. (1895) *Studies on Hysteria*, Standard Edition II. London: Hogarth Press.

Esterson, A. (2001) 'The mythologizing of psychoanalytic history: deception and self-deception in Freud's accounts of the seduction theory episode' *History of Psychiatry* 12(3): 329–352.

Freud, S. (1900) *The Interpretation of Dreams*, SE V. London: Hogarth Press.

Freud, S. (1915) *The Unconscious*, SE XIV. London: Hogarth Press.

Freud, S. & Breuer, J. (1895) *Studies on Hysteria, Preface to the First Edition*, SE II. London: Hogarth Press.

Freud, S. & Breuer, J. (1896) *The Aetiology of Hysteria*, SE II. London: Hogarth Press.

Freud, S. & Breuer, J. (1918) *Studies on Hysteria, Preface to the Second Edition*, SE II. London: Hogarth Press.

Gay, P. (1988) *Freud, A Life for Our Time*. London: J.M. Dent and Sons.

Grosskurth, P. (1986) *Melanie Klein: Her World and Her Work*. London: Macmillan.

Haidt, J. (2012) *The Righteous Mind*. London: Penguin Books.

Hoggett, P. (2018) 'Ressentiment and Grievance' *British Journal of Psychotherapy* 34 (3): 303–407.

Krafft-Ebing, R. (1896) *Psychopathia Sexualis*, Internet Archive HTML5 Uploader 1.2.

Lacan, J. (1968) *The Seminars of Jacques Lacan, Seminar XVI D'un Autre à l'autre*. Paris: Seuil.

Lamb, W. (2020) 2nd Viscount Melbourne. *Biographies net*. STANDS4 LLC. Web. www.biographies.net/people/en/william_lamb_2nd_viscount_melbourne

Masson, J. (Ed.) (1985) *The Complete Letters of Sigmund Freud to Wilhelm Fliess, 1887–1904*. Cambridge, MA and London: The Belknap Press.

Masson, J. (1992) *Final Analysis*. London: Fontana.

Sinasson, V. (1995) 'Anne Marie Sandler, Director of the Anna Freud Centre from 1994' *Journal of Child Psychotherapy* 21(3): 360–374.

Sulloway, F. (1992) *Freud, Biologist of the Mind*. Harvard: University Press.

Tetlock, P.E. (2002) 'Social functionalist frameworks for judgment and choice: intuitive politicians, theologians and prosecutors' *Psychological Review* 109: 451–457.

Wason, P.C. (1960) 'On the failure to eliminate hypotheses in a conceptual task' *Quarterly Journal of Experimental Psychology* 12: 129–140.

Webster, R. (1996) *Why Freud Was Wrong: Sin, Science and Psychoanalysis*. London: Harper Collins.

Chapter 6

Certainty in depression

In sooth I know not why I am so sad
It wearies me; you say it wearies you
But how I caught it, found it, came by it
What stuff 'tis made of, whereof it is born
I am to learn.

William Shakespeare,
The Merchant of Venice, Ii

In *The Merchant of Venice*, Antonio is a wealthy merchant who is chronic-
ally depressed. Antonio captures the nature of depression and the inability
of the sufferer to explain the reason for it. This chapter will take as its
focus the human problem of depression, its causes and its treatment. One
of the most painful aspects of depression is the measure of certainty and
conviction that the depressed person feels. Anyone who has known
a sufferer knows that attempts to convince them that things are not as bad
as they think do not often work. There are convictions in most depressed
people that need to be subjected to thought. This thinking will take time
and effort but will help to release an individual from this state. Depression
is a complex human condition meaning something specific to each individual. In order to find a solid piece of ground from which to begin to consider it, we can think of it as the condition of a person who has lost
someone or something.

Bereavement is perhaps the most agonising mental pain of normal
human experience. It has a trajectory and grows less acute for most people
as time passes. For the clinician, bereavement can clarify what the primary
loss has been but that does not mean that the work stops there. The res-
idues of all sorts of losses will flow into the main channel of the primary
loss and the work of therapy will often be to identify some of the other
losses.

Nevertheless, in bereavement the main task is to accept and learn to
live with the terrible certainty of the finality of death. Before the

certainty of the loss can be accepted, a new certainty is often wanted. This may involve blame or anger. The person who is blamed is often a doctor or emergency responder but the pursuit of what the survivors think is justice can become a vendetta of serious proportions. As is often the case with the death of a young person or deaths caused by tragic accidents, the survivors may seek to find the solid ground of certainty by setting up a charity to make sure that whatever is blamed as the cause of the death 'will never happen again'. Setting this up is a positive action and also softens the certainty of loss. The name at least of the deceased person will live on. Setting up the new certainty may lay bare old resentments or fears of rejection and not being loved enough. It may involve the conviction of having been neglected or ignored in a Will. Working with these reactions may seem very difficult because of the total conviction of the bereaved.

Looking at the standard views of depression, the theory to be considered will focus on Aaron Beck's well-known study of the treatment of depression leading to his *Depression Inventory* (Beck 1972) and Richard Layard's promotion of the Cognitive Behavioural Therapy movement, looking at the research since and the public and professional reactions to the research (Layard 2006). Aaron Beck brought the thinking of many writers together in his questionnaire, which establishes the severity of depression. He did much more than that, as the questions indicated that the thinking of the person suffering from clinical depression is faulty. They have a skewed view of reality, their own and that of others. He or she can learn to think differently and from this hypothesis arises the power of Cognitive Behavioural Therapy. Beck did much to show the phenomenology of depression and the extent to which sufferers seek confidence and certainty in their suffering.

What exactly is depression?

Like much else in psychotherapy, the study of depression is made more difficult because 'depression' is a word in common everyday use and has become blurred around the edges. Psychological professionals of course distinguish between sadness as for example in bereavement and the full horror of the depression expressed by the twentieth-century poet Gerard Manley Hopkins:

> No worst there is none. Pitched past pitch of grief,
> More pangs will, schooled at fore pangs, wilder wring.
>
> (Hopkins 1985)

That is clinical depression. Perhaps even worse than grief is the lethargy of depression: 'I cannot get up. I cannot do anything. Anyway, nothing is worth doing'. The American Psychiatric Association lists the following factors:

- feeling sad or having a depressed mood
- loss of interest or pleasure in activities once enjoyed
- changes in appetite – weight loss or gain unrelated to dieting
- trouble sleeping or sleeping too much
- loss of energy or increased fatigue
- increase in purposeless physical activity (e.g., hand-wringing or pacing) or slowed movements and speech (actions observable by others)
- feeling worthless or guilty
- difficulty thinking, concentrating or making decisions
- thoughts of death or suicide.

The NHS has a similar list:

- continuous low mood or sadness
- feeling hopeless and helpless
- having low self-esteem
- feeling tearful
- feeling guilt-ridden
- feeling irritable and intolerant of others
- having no motivation or interest in things
- finding it difficult to make decisions
- not getting any enjoyment out of life
- feeling anxious or worried
- having suicidal thoughts or thoughts of harming.

Both emphasise that for low mood to become clinical depression it must last for a minimum of two weeks at a time. This distinguishes it from the fluctuation in moods which any individual is likely to experience. Both these lists emphasise how painful the experience of depression can be. One of the main themes of this book therefore is how conviction can be used as a defence against the experience of other feelings and thoughts. We might expect that a rigid adherence to fundamentalist religion or hero worship of a cult leader might be examples of defences against disastrous forms of depression.

The novel discussed in previous chapters, *A Song for Issy Bradley* (Bray 2014), shows the impact of the death of four-year-old Issy from meningitis. Her father, Ian, is a Mormon bishop and at first is confident that he can 'bless her to live'. He speaks the words of the blessing in the full belief that he can save Issy but her mother, Claire is not able to do anything other than repeat 'please' over and over in her mind. Ian then has to watch his child die. This does not seem to shake his faith, which becomes more certain and more dogmatic. He will not allow his children any doubt or questioning. But what his wife cannot forgive is that he says in his prayer at the bedside of the dying child, 'You have been blessed with a special mother whom your Heavenly Father loves and according to her great faith I bless you to be healed ...'. He has made Issy's recovery contingent on Claire's faith and she doesn't know how she will ever forgive him (Bray 2014: 79). In this way the anger that underlies Claire's depression begins. She watches Ian who gradually understands that there is no hope any longer 'the dip of his shoulders marks the retreat of his certainty' (2014: 81).

After Issy's death it is Ian's job to help his family with their grief. He is so overwhelmed himself that he cannot speak when on the telephone to give a message to be delivered to his parents who are in Dublin on their mission to make converts. They decide not to come even to the funeral and Ian is disappointed and left alone with his own family. Each Monday as Mormons they have Family Home Evening and Ian manages to convince himself that everything will be all right: 'There's something about saying words out loud that makes them true and having explained things to everyone he finds himself converted' (Bray 2014: 92). Ian is able to feel certain of his religion and of the comfort that they can all receive by believing in Heavenly Father. He puts his foot down about the funeral. Claire would like to make a slide show of pictures of Issy but Ian is able to assert his authority by saying 'It's not allowed' after he looks it up in his Church Handbook. His argument is that he cannot make allowances for his own family and set a precedent but underneath there seems to be a conviction that he must be definite. He must know something. Jacob the younger son admires his certainty: 'I'm glad you know stuff, Dad' (Bray 2014: 93).

In the description of Family Home Evening we are shown the process of certainty reasserting itself in the face of the terrible certainty of loss. Ian is able to convince himself of his own religious belief and can even find a way of understanding that he blessed Issy to live but she still died. His own father had said in the face of this difficulty that she was blessed to live and that might not mean living in the sense of staying in this world. He struggles against his own grief but gradually manages to use his texts from the book of Mormon to convince himself that 'Heavenly Father' had a special purpose for little Issy. His own mother and father seem to have no doubt that they are right to decide not to come home because of baptising a convert the next week. He is able to remember his father's teaching and he can immerse himself back in his fundamentalist faith and cease to show how destabilised he is by the death of his child. Ian tries to manage without grieving and so leaves his wife alone.

We have a picture of the misery of depression in his wife, Claire. She was not a Mormon originally and we are told that she has married Ian but has her doubts about the whole structure of beliefs and practices. Conversion in order to marry an adherent of an extreme group is also the theme of Michael Arditti's novel about Jewish fundamentalism *The Enemy of the Good* (Arditti 2009). Such conversions, however sincerely undertaken, can cause great difficulties both for the families concerned and for the individual herself. Each of Claire's surviving children has his or her own doubts and difficulties. Jacob tries to bring about a miracle because his father has convinced him that enough faith can be sufficient to bring his sister back. Claire is the one who submits to a grief reaction, which becomes severe depression. She is very much alone, retreating to Issy's bed where she breathes in the smell and sensation of the child's presence and she will not get up or speak to anyone. She stays there in spite of the pleas of her husband who is struggling to look after the family and keep going with his job teaching maths and managing the Mormons for whom he is responsible as their bishop.

Depression with no obvious bereavement

Grief is a clear reason for the kind of depression arising from a known loss. In some cases, there is no apparent loss at all. Very often analytic work uncovers the loss or losses that lead to this state but they may be deeply unconscious. This state of mind is known as clinical or non-reactive depression. It is an area of mental ill health that is known to respond to medication. Each patient is different of course but most respond within a few weeks and will feel some benefit. Research has shown benefits and the NHS therefor recommends a combination of medication and talking therapy for mild to moderate depression. Many people would prefer to be cured by medication alone. This may be caused by the wish to retain one's convictions and yet get rid of them pharmacologically. This paradoxical position seems necessary to some sufferers because some of the main elements of depression are damaging convictions.

Richard Layard wrote a highly influential report on depression in the UK in 2006. The *Depression Report* singled out and recommended only Cognitive Behavioural Therapy for the treatment of mild to moderate depression. This caused some argument and distress in the field of psychotherapy among those who practise other models. As time has gone by, the therapy world has allowed some changes but does not seem to have lost any of the major models since then. In the *Report*, Layard (2006) argued that the prevalence of depression at the level of mild to moderate was such that there was need for action from a humanitarian point of view. He went on to argue that Cognitive Behavioural Therapy could be delivered over six to eight weeks by a therapist who could be inexperienced or in some sort of training. With this plan, the cost of a national programme could be easily recouped from the saving in increased ability to work.

Layard researched his subject well. He put figures to both the problem and the cost of remedying it. According to him the incidence of depression at this level is at 40% likelihood during a lifetime for any individual. It will affect one in six of the population at any time. He gave a figure of £750 as the cost of providing treatment on the National Health Service in 2006. Such was his faith in the efficacy of Cognitive Behavioural Therapy that he believed that damaging beliefs and certainties could be challenged and that process would unlock the mental and emotional prison of depression.

Depression: illness or psychological problem?

In *The New Black: Mourning, Melancholia and Depression* the psychoanalyst Darian Leader (2008) argues against seeing depression as an illness with a pharmaceutical cure. This argument is necessary because the first area of certainty that we encounter in the consideration of depression is the belief that it is a problem arising in the physical brain, which can be cured by tinkering with the level of serotonin. This is of course supported by the companies producing the drugs that alter serotonin uptake. A financial imperative grows under this basic position and, as Leader points out, certainly does not encourage any impulse to examine closely the nature of the concept of depression itself, let alone its causes and best treatment. He goes as far as to assert that depression is an artificial illness created to describe what anti-depressants cure (2008: 12).

Like many psychotherapists, Leader turns instead to the myriad human stories of loss and bereavement that are implicated. He understands that the depressed person is suffering from a variety of symptoms that derive from complex and always different human stories.

Where the neurotic person may feel inferior to others and inadequate, the melancholic will actually accuse himself of worthlessness as if his life itself were some kind of sin or crime. He doesn't just feel inadequate; he *knows* he is inadequate. There is certainty here rather than doubt (2008: 35).

A very different approach was taken by the *Diagnostic and Statistical Manual V* (2000), in which 'Prolonged Grief' was taken as a pathological condition. This gave rise to objections from those who believe that grief is a normal and a necessary human reaction to loss. There is perhaps some value in highlighting a prolonged and painful grief reaction that allows for no movement or change at all. The argument has made us all recognise how individual and human this condition is. Searching for definitive distinctions between depression and grief leads to no very firm conclusions but to Venn diagrams in which there is considerable overlap of symptoms like anger and a sense of pointlessness. There are some areas of grief that lie outside the circle of depression: yearning, sadness, longing for the return of the lost one would be there.

Leader discusses the lack of success of research in explaining or resolving the problems of depression. He sees that one road to understanding depression is to look at the whole field of literature. Stories tell us about loss and grief and mourning and the consequent suffering of mothers, fathers, siblings, lovers and friends from Sophocles' Antigone to Winston Smith in George Orwell's novel *1984*. Severe grief reactions can look very like depression. There is no distinction in levels of severity.

Miss Havisham in *Great Expectations*, the novel by Charles Dickens (1861), lost her lover who jilted her on her wedding day. She is shown to us as extremely depressed. She sits in her rotting wedding dress surrounded by the crumbling remains of the wedding breakfast. Moreover, she is so angry that she seeks to punish all males for the crime that was perpetrated against her when she was abandoned. Her grief reaction has not become mourning but has become depression. Yet her depression is unique and not only because Dickens has dramatised it into something verging on a caricature. Miss Havisham does not seem to find life pointless. Revenge has become her purpose and she wants to punish the young boy Pip by seeing him hopelessly in love with her beautiful niece, Estella, who will break his heart.

Miss Havisham clearly is very angry. She does not express anger directly but her desire for revenge appears to be enough to keep her alive. All of that is characteristic of what we might call depression and of course she is not exactly like any other depressive. Just as Leader says, she has her own specific and, of course in this case, fictional depression.

Yet Miss Havisham has certainly lost someone and her depression might be considered to be a case of pathological grief. One of the distinctions here might be lack of longing for the lost one. She shows no sign of wanting her fiancé back even if that were possible. She has a space in her mind that she has filled with anger and the desire for vengeance. Dickens is superb story-teller but he makes no attempt to tell us what might have gone on the mind of this woman. Like the witches in Shakespeare's *Macbeth* who never tell him to murder the King, Miss Havisham never told Pip that she was the one who wanted him to be a gentleman. His own mind was only too ready to believe the false narrative that unwound.

Miss Havisham also shows how the depressive uses inanimate objects or things. She sits surrounded by the objects that were to celebrate her happiness in marrying. Their decay and mould demonstrate the decay of her own hope and ultimately of her mind.

The depressive that we see in the consulting room often wishes other people to see the state of hopelessness. She may fail exams or drop out of college. She may berate herself for this sort of failure. Alternatively, she may simply shrug it off as unimportant because she is unimportant. She may also know that she is poised dangerously above a seething well of anger into which she could easily pull others who are important to her.

Seeing this led therapists to the view that depression is 'anger turned against the self'. There may be an element of truth in this: it was Freud's view in his famous statement in *Mourning and Melancholia*: 'The shadow of the object falls upon the ego' (Freud 1917). What Freud meant was that the depressed person treats himself with the anger that he might have felt about the lost person. For this reason, depression often involves various forms of failure and self-sabotage. In the case of Miss Havisham, we can see that the original loss clearly implies that she has failed to be a bride. She stays half in and half out of the role of bride. However, she refuses to give it up clinging to the remnants of what has irrevocably gone.

Grief and anger together can equal depression

Perhaps the clearest illustration of someone seeking certainty in order to manage loss is Shakespeare's Hamlet. He is already grieving the loss of his father at the beginning of the play. The arrival of his father's ghost prevents him from moving on with his grief to a more balanced position of sadness. The ghost makes him angry but it also makes him depressed. He is tempted not to believe in the ghost but has to accept that other people have seen it. Even so, he cannot act and that is partly because his enemy is now his stepfather, the King, who has all the spies and actors of the Danish State at his disposal. In Hamlet's agonising we see how the pain of depression prevents action, which the person knows he wants or needs to carry out. For most people, it is more often a matter of getting up and going to work than avenging a death by killing a king, but the feeling of self-hatred can be equally intense.

Hamlet's soliloquies show that Shakespeare knew something of the terrible self-loathing of the depressed person who partly wants to act and partly refuses. Like his father who was killed while sleeping, Hamlet feels passive and inadequate. He also shows us how depression ruins relationships. Anger spills over and is displaced from his mother onto poor Ophelia. She has no idea what is happening to her and is in any case under the orders of her father.

For Hamlet, anger and hatred are powerful realities. These feeling envelop his mother and his love for Ophelia but the strongest expression of anger is reserved for himself:

> What should such fellows as I do, crawling between earth and heaven? We are arrant knaves, all. Believe none of us. Go thy ways to a nunnery.
>
> (*Hamlet*, Act III, scene i)

The depressed person cannot bear the burden of another person. Hamlet sends Ophelia off to a place of safety, where her virtue will be protected from such 'arrant knaves' as he feels he is. In fact, of course, he sends her off to her suicide. The position of the other person is often unbearable. They can neither help not leave the suffering one to their hurt and anger. They may well become irrelevant, just a nuisance to be flicked away. This is a position of self-hatred that cannot usually be shifted by any declarations of love or of the worth of the depressed person and for this reason the partner may well become reactively depressed. In Hamlet's case, the loss is clear even though he is anxious for his friend to corroborate what he has seen. For many depressed people it is not easy to see what they have lost but patient work in therapy finds both loss and anger at some level.

Since physical objects can be linked to symptoms it pays a therapist to examine the objects closely. They are a way of showing other people what has happened and the suffering that is being endured. Because they are things, they are immutable and hold the position of certainties. In *Great Expectations*, the fiancée has long gone but the evidence of loss and anger remain. The ruins of Miss Havisham's wedding cake still exist and its decay represents an internal decay of her capacity for pity and love. She demonstrates the decay of what might have been maternal feelings in her treatment of the boy Pip when she commands him to 'Play, boy, play'. This is an impossible command to obey, as true play is spontaneous and arises from the child's own nature, not an external admonition. In any case, the child is terrified and is filled with his reaction to the scene in front of him. This perversion of Miss Havisham's pre-existing self is a demonstration of the fixation to a loss that we might see as characteristic of depression.

Turning to the toxic effect of certainty in the patient in a consulting room, we can see how people create less dramatic versions of Miss Havisham's wedding breakfast for themselves. I saw a patient Maureen who was a single woman aged 35. She came to see me, referred by her General Practitioner. She was taking anti-depressants and she assured me that she had been depressed since she was 13. This had been made worse because recently, after saying goodbye to her boyfriend one night, she rang him up the next day to say that she did not want to see him any more. 'Why did I do that? I was just suddenly sure that the relationship would make us both sad. But there was no real reason. I'm just stupid'. Her childhood had been happy and she hoped that I would not want her to blame her parents for anything. I asked her what had happened when she was 13 to make her become depressed. Nothing at all, except that she had reached puberty and begun menstruating and, oh, she had also understood that she was going to boarding school the next year. But she wasn't sad about either of these things Her elder sister had already attended the school that she would go to and she was proud to be old enough. She was also proud to have 'achieved womanhood'.

I noted the possible seeds of distress in this brave account but did not seek to disrupt it at that point. I just asked her about how school was when she arrived. To my surprise she hesitated and started mopping tears. 'I wanted to tell you about my cubicle at school and how much I enjoyed learning Latin and Physics so that I could talk to Father'. I already knew that her father was an academic.

> But I can't help remembering the first day, when my parents dropped me off at school. They drove off down the driveway and I realised that I would be there for half a term before I would see them again. They didn't seem to mind. I did. But I didn't tell them, so how could they know?

My Mother told me years later that she cried all the way home in the car, but I didn't know that then. She just told me because we were listening to a programme about boarding schools and the damage that they can do. I think she wanted me to know that it did damage to her too. She said that

> she thought I would be all right because my sister was there. My sister ignored me. I don't think she wanted to remember what it was like when you first begin. Of course, I don't blame her. She began at eight so she was much worse off than I was. It makes me cry to think how hard it was for my parents to scrape together the fees for both of us. But they wanted to be fair to me because they thought it was such a great good thing for both of us.

As Maureen's therapist, I could see the importance of this ambiguous experience. I could see how she wiped her eyes, sat up straight and began to tell me how much her parents had done for her. My concerns were both that she needed this valuing of her parents but also that I had to bear in mind that she was suffering from depression that limited her pleasure in life. I could see that there were two losses that I knew about already. In being taken off to boarding school Maureen might have felt that she was losing her childhood and with it her automatic right to the presence and attention of her parents. Without any choice in the matter, Maureen seemed to have felt that she was pushed into a second weaning experience.

Another aspect of the experience of loss at 13 was the onset of puberty. Maureen was explicitly calling this a gain to be proud of. At the same time, like most other girls of her age, she probably felt ambivalent about it: she was gaining maturity and losing childhood. The two experiences of loss had led Maureen to develop a carapace. Her parents had done everything to show that they loved her and were sending her to school entirely for her own good. But the depressive fear that they wanted to get rid of her so that they could go off together in the car and have their Oedipal drama uninterrupted by their daughter was to be kept at bay. Once she had managed to overcome the tears at night in her cubicle, she did not want to think about it any more. She said that her sister did not want to think about it, and the same applied just as much to her.

All this enabled me to help her to some sort of recognition of her sadness and bereavement but it left her present distress untouched. She had found a boyfriend but she had, in her own words, sabotaged the feelings that they both had for each other. This was another aspect of depression to be considered. I wanted to know in what way she 'sabotaged' the good feelings between them. She told me that she thought she smothered him. She was constantly asking him whether he was all right. She worried that she was not enough for him. She worried that she was ugly and he would find a better-looking girl. I supposed that if he was going to find a better-looking girl anyway, she might as well end the relationship. She glared at me and said, 'Well, he might find someone else, but he only might and that could also mean that he also might not'. Without any further input from me, she had arrived at the necessary doubt. This might look easy to achieve but of course the doubts about the depressed person's own merits are very difficult to shift. They become certainties: 'I am ugly. I am not worth anything. What happens to me is of no importance to anyone'. Beneath this of course is the conviction that 'What happens to me is of great importance to me. I want you to reassure me and, if you don't, that will be the cause of my depression'.

The danger of conviction of helplessness

Claire in the story of Issy Bradley retreats to bed unable to bear the immense loss of her little daughter to meningitis. She dreams that the sea is hurtling up the beach towards the two of them and she will not be able to save Issy from it (Bray 2014: 292). This is the powerlessness of depression and is of course related to the hopelessness of loss. She was not able to save her child from the ravages of meningitis and in the present of the novel she cannot save herself or her family. Carys Bray interweaves misunderstandings that prevent the family members from helping each other. Ian, the father would like to protect his younger son Jacob from the pain of seeing that Issy's goldfish has died. He hastens to replace it and Jacob is able to believe that he has brought about a miracle by praying as he has been taught. This leads to a pinnacle of hope for the child and then of course disillusionment when he finds out that his father has bought a new goldfish to replace the dead one. For Jacob, one aspect of avoiding long-term depression is renouncing the certainty of religious faith in order to face the sadness that he cannot have his sister returned to him. When he knows that his father had replaced the goldfish and it has not been resurrected, he sinks: 'Oh dear, he says, Oh dear. He is lost like Hansel, all his breadcrumbs have been eaten and he doesn't know how he will ever get Issy home' (Bray 2014: 344).

Religious faith seems to provide a form of certainty, which can be a defence against depression. Jacob however demonstrates the caveats that there must inevitably be in such a defence. His father, Ian, is disturbed and caught off guard by the needs of his family for some kind of help with conviction although none of them asks for it overtly. Jacob takes everything that he has been taught about 'Heavenly Father' and the possibility of miracles and resurrection quite literally but he has to learn that this faith is not all that it seems. Ian has no answers other than that one day he'll understand. This seems to imply that such faith is not to be taken literally and that adults will make various modifications to it in their own minds. Doubt is inevitable but painful.

Helplessness transforms to anger

Damaging certainty in depression is shown most vividly in the mother, Claire, who was not a Mormon to begin with and has less certainty in the Church than she has in her husband. The emotion that grips her is anger, which is never expressed as such. Lying in Issy's bed, she makes her husband suffer greatly. He has to manage the family in all the practical ways: doing the washing, making the sandwiches and so on. But the greatest punishment that she imposes is on his effectiveness as a husband and as a bishop. If his wife is unable to show certainty in faith, he will suffer from the disapproval of the other men and may even be removed from his position as bishop, a fearful humiliation. She never says that she wants this, but by refusing to get up and help him she shows how angry she is that he made Issy's life depend on her faith in his blessing. When a small deputation of men comes to visit Ian and check up on the situation, Claire does get out of bed and comes downstairs to meet them looking as though she might be physically ill but showing clearly that she hasn't washed for some time. Her appearance adds to Ian's shame and is part of a need to punish him although we have no idea whether that is a conscious desire or unconscious impulse.

In the end, Claire goes to the beach and, as the tide comes in, she lets the waves take her and overwhelm her. The grief in her case cannot be accepted but takes her away from her family. No-one was able to take away from Claire the conviction that she could not survive the guilt of having been unable to save her child. The novel shows us the mistakes that her family made, especially her husband, but does not offer any certainty that a different approach would have been enough. In fact, the desolation of loss is shown to be so distressing as to be harmful in itself. All of them suffer but for the children and for Ian, the suffering is in trying to restore something that is lost. Guilt is a common burden in grief but Alma, the oldest who takes his mother's saved money on impulse suffers considerable guilt over it but in the end is able to find a way of restoring it. Claire, on the other hand, is not able to find any way of managing her guilt at not having enough faith to bring about the miracle that saving her daughter's life would have been. But even more difficult for her is managing her anger with her husband for putting her in a painful dilemma: either she accepts the certainty of her husband's faith in which case she is to blame or she doubts that framework on which she has based the whole of her married life. The result is that she has to withdraw like Miss Havisham, unable to reconcile these positions.

The case of Claire shows the power of repressed anger to cause suffering for both its possessor and those around. Men of course can also be subject to this problem. Ludo is a young man of 34 in a successful role as a junior manager in a branch of a large company. His parents are Polish and came to this country before he was born. He tells me that it was very important to them that he should perform well at school so that they would feel that they had made the right decision in coming here. He and his younger sister both managed to achieve well at school and his parents were pleased. He followed the designated path and went to a middle-range university and then got a traineeship in the company where he still works.

His problem is that two years ago he became depressed, saw no point in anything and left his job. For a while he just stayed in bed. Because he maintained a presence on social media, a friend from school came to see him and he decided to get up. He went on a belated gap year and worked for a time in a project, building a school in central Africa. He said that for a time he felt much better. He returned to England and was overwhelmed by the same depressive feelings as before.

I asked him what he thought was waiting for him here. 'Well my parents', he said. 'They were disappointed by me. My Dad said that I was no good. I couldn't stay with my job and I couldn't settle to anything else. I didn't even have a girlfriend'. He told me that his GP had prescribed anti-depressants, which he was taking. He went on to tell me that his original company had taken him back. He was grateful for that but he was finding the work more difficult than he expected.

We are so short staffed that I have to stay late every night and sometimes have to work weekends. I know other people have to do that sort of thing but it isn't necessary. It's because the senior management is too preoccupied with profit to pay for enough staff. My boss is hopeless. He just says that he can see it's a problem but he does nothing to improve it.

Ludo settled into a habit of talking about this boss and his refusal to help with what sounded like a very frustrating and tiring overload. I put it to him that, in spite of his patient and resigned way of telling me about it, he was actually just as angry with his boss as he might have been with his father. Neither could be satisfied. The company seemed to have turned into a parent who could never be pleased but would always ask for more. Seeing that this was so, he began to express some anger and went through a period in which he expressed both anger and his sadness at not being able to be the son that was wanted.

Anger was not the only key to shifting Ludo's depression but it was an important element. He had, like most people, feared that his anger would do so much damage that it could not be risked. I was aware that at that stage he was still only talking about anger but, as time went by, I became more aware that his anger was spilling over into relationships with friends, although never entering into the session with me. Clearly, he needed to keep his feelings in check at work and maybe with his parents too. At least he was able to hear himself saying aloud that he had grounds for anger and was not required to repress it in his own mind.

Making anger work

As always, a new adaptation to external conditions that were undoubtedly difficult required giving up some reassuring certainty. Ludo had to accommodate a father and a boss who he could imagine enduring his anger and still being available to him as male figures of strength and goodness. I came to understand that by risking being angry with them he was also risking weakening them. If they did not retaliate and hurt him it might be because they were not able to. His fear was less of retaliation than of castration. This intimate connection between certainty and castration is vital to understand particularly, but not only, in men. This leads to another even more difficult understanding, which is that the danger is internal as well as external. At the most obvious level, we have men who come to us wanting to limit or restrain their anger and for them, the fear that this process will be castrating is obvious. Beyond this is the fear of disabling parts of the self.

Melanie Klein (1946: 9) understood the need to manage the different elements in the mind, which she referred to as internal objects. Most people can accept that they speak to themselves and that the voices that they use can be different. Some are the voices of the people who have loved or been good to the individual and some are hostile and full of hate and anger. Keeping a balance between them and not becoming totally convinced by one or the other is part of the work of therapy. First the different voices need to be heard and recognised. Ludo need to understand the extent to which he felt the need to defend himself from the disempowerment which his powerful male figures threatened. Then he was able to choose what sort of man he wanted to be. Of course, he could not achieve it all at once. He would spend his life pursuing a goal but he at least had some idea of what the goal was.

Freedom from depression

People attend therapy sessions to help them with prolonged grief and also for what they see as unexplained depression. The task of the therapist is to uncover the hidden convictions that each person has acquired for himself. He may have lost someone and cannot express anger with the lost person for going even in his own head. He may then punish the lost one in effigy but we discover that the effigy is of himself. Often it takes someone else to see this. He cannot see it for himself. In any case mourning needs help. We have funerals and rituals to help in the sense that the loss is shared. They also help towards the necessary belief that the lost one has really gone. In this way they help to achieve the certainty of loss and at the same time to make it a little more bearable. Many of the other losses of human life will share some of the characteristics of bereavement but will not be socially accepted as being the same and only a therapist may take seriously the loss of work in retirement or of a much-loved animal. Human beings are capable of love and therefore they suffer in losses of all sorts. Discovering and loosening the accompanying convictions may help in the process of moving on.

References

Arditti, M. (2009) *The Enemy of the Good*. London: Arcadia Books.

Beck, A.T. (1972) *Depression: Causes and Treatment*. Philadelphia: University of Pennsylvania Press.

Bray, C. (2014) *A Song for Issy Bradley*. London: Hutchinson.

Diagnostic and Statistical Manual (DSM) V. (2000) 'Diagnostic and statistical manual' *Neuroscience & Biobehavioral Reviews* 24(3): 355–364.

Dickens, C. (1861) *Great Expectations*. London: Chapman and Hall.

Freud, S. (1917) *Mourning and Melancholia*, SE 14. London: Hogarth Press.

Hopkins, G.M. (1985) *Gerard Manley Hopkins: Poems and Prose*. Harmondsworth: Penguin Classics.

Klein, M. (1946) 'Notes on some schizoid mechanisms' in Klein, M. (Ed.), (1984), *Envy and Gratitude* (pp. 1–24). London: Hogarth Press.

Layard, R. (2006) *The Depression Report*. London: The Centre for Economic Performance's Mental Health Policy Group.

Leader, D. (2008) *The New Black: Mourning, Melancholia and Depression*. Harmondsworth: Penguin.

Schaverien, J. (2011) 'Boarding school syndrome: broken attachments, a hidden trauma' *British Journal of Psychotherapy* 27(2): 138–155.

Chapter 7

Certainty on the autistic spectrum

Philip is a middle-aged man of 39. He came to see a therapist because he was having problems at work. He worked in Information Technology where he felt that he had much to offer. However, his boss was requiring that he join his work colleagues in the department once a month at the pub after work on a Friday, 'just for half an hour so that we can get to know each other better'. Philip said that he was willing to do all the work required of him, but going out with the others was a complete waste of time and he could not understand why anyone would want to do it, let alone try to make others do it. He left this job two weeks after his first session.

Philip told his therapist that he had left four other jobs in the previous year because he found the habits of some of his colleagues difficult, for one reason or another. One had talked too much and another always jumped up when she had finished a piece of work with exclamations of satisfaction. Philip felt out of place: he believed that no matter how he tried to fit in, they would talk about him, criticising his work.

On investigating a bit further, the therapist was struck by the number of endings and partings in his life. He was from a family of teachers. His father had wanted him to continue a family tradition and had sent Philip to the same boarding school that he had attended, although he had apparently not enjoyed it at all. Philip also hated it and recalled that the journey there each term was 'the worst part'. He could not say why. When the therapist commented that perhaps he was sad about the impending separation he merely said 'probably'. He was remarkably precise in dating the events of his life. He quoted the day and date of his first arrival at the school. It seemed to have impressed itself on him with strong but unidentified feelings.

Philip described his education. He had been expelled from the first boarding school but was sent to another where he completed the exams necessary to begin a university course. He dropped out of university and went home. His parents seem to have accepted this ending but encouraged him to find a course in computer games technology, which he was able to complete. He then found work in IT. He told the therapist 'I decided just to be a geek and accept my fate'.

Philip was still living at home and had no long-term girlfriends. He liked routines and his parents led very predictable lives, although for both of them retirement was imminent. The therapist discovered that he hated the breaks when she could not see him. He would never attend the last session before a break. He would not say that he minded her absence, but always gave some reason for his absence that was connected with his health.

The autistic spectrum

Philip clearly had characteristics of autism. This is an area of mental functioning where there is often profound unhappiness partly because people see themselves and are seen by others as 'not normal'. In autism, there is a spectrum of characteristics that range from geekiness, or an intense interest in things, to difficulties in social interaction, communication and imagination. These are the difficulties. There are also advantages from positive abilities and qualities.

This chapter will consider the part played by the need for certainty in autism in the form of predictability. This need is prominent both in the suffering itself and in the treatment methods that have been used to help. Questioning these certainties is vital for the self-respect of the people in this position and for the effectiveness of any help that is given Most of this discussion will apply to people in high-functioning autistic states. People in this position are said to have Asperger's syndrome. Often, but by no means always, male, they usually have a high intelligence score and good verbal skills but they have all sorts of difficulties in social communication and therefore at work. Illustrations will be taken from the practise of psychotherapy in a university where there are brilliant academics, often mathematicians and scientists, with distressing emotional lives. Illustrations will also be taken from fiction such as *The Rosie Project* by Graeme Simsion (2013).

The American *Diagnostic and Statistical Manual* (DSM V 2018) defines autism spectrum disorder as 'persistent difficulties with social communication and social interaction' and 'restricted and repetitive patterns of behaviours, activities or interests' (this includes sensory behaviour), present since early childhood, to the extent that these patterns 'limit and impair everyday functioning'. Such a definition forms a starting point for any discussion but leaves out all the human suffering as well as the potential value of some of these qualities of mind.

'He's on the spectrum' has become part of common speech to describe someone who behaves in a difficult way. It is almost as much used as 'he's bipolar'. Shortening the full expressions leads to something that doesn't make much sense; it is a label quoted with great confidence but with little knowledge of what the terms mean. It is useful to speak of a spectrum of autistic disorder because the phenomena certainly come in various degrees of severity and with a sprinkling of symptoms but rarely the full range of possibilities. People who are not 'on the spectrum' are known as 'neurotypicals'. As someone from the neurotypical group, I have to try to understand the problems of those 'on the spectrum' whose brains function in a slightly different way from mine. There are certainly problems but there are also benefits. In this chapter, while looking at the benefits, I will also consider the problems that arise in so far as they are caused by fear and a need for certainty.

An autistic person finds human behaviour profoundly puzzling at times, although his cognitive ability can enable him to hide this sense of alienation. Such a person feels the need to be confident about some things since relationships with other people give him a sense of anxiety. Other people are unpredictable, illogical and sometimes incomprehensible. Understanding the anxiety and its cause goes some way to a better understanding of the obsessional and magical thinking that often accompanies this system of thought.

Magical thinking is often an aspect of obsessional states and carries with it a quality of certainty that can be lying hidden in every person's mind, not just those with Asperger's syndrome. A speaker at a conference carried out an interesting experiment before giving a paper on this subject. The audience were asked to write down the name of someone they loved. Then they were asked to write underneath the name the sentence 'I hope this person dies'. No-one would do it. All sorts of reasons were given, mainly that it would not be true. The speaker had never said that what was to be written was true: it had been set out as an experiment. The total inhibition felt by most people in the audience seems to have arisen from fear of appearing to oneself to wish for something and fear that this would magically make it happen.

Philip does not appear to have any strong indications in this direction and yet he had certain rules about colours: the rules had an almost magical significance for him. The therapist noticed that he wore brightly coloured socks. One Tuesday, with embarrassment, he said to her that he had to wear the wrong socks because he had lost one of his Tuesday pair. He had had to put on the socks that were meant for Wednesday. The ritual that connected socks and days of the week turned out to be his insurance for good fortune although he was not able to say for certain what he thought he could achieve if he followed the rule or what would go wrong if he did not. He just felt better if he did.

One of the aspects of this exchange was that the therapist became more than usually aware of how Philip expected his thoughts to be met with scorn. He knew that 'normal' people did not care about the colour of their socks as much as he did. However, while he expected to be met with derision, he clearly felt that his perspective was important and true. The therapist wondered whether his parents would have sympathised with this need but decided not to ask at that moment in case the answer led to further recollections of humiliation. Later, Philip was able to say that his father found some of his habits very odd and would get impatient with him. He said that he thought he had begun his 'habits' at boarding school when he was bewildered by having 'too many people' in his dormitory.

Philip did not demonstrate other markedly obsessional behaviour but he said several times that he liked living with his parents because they had settled routines that he could join. He liked going to the supermarket with his mother. She appreciated his help in carrying the shopping out to the car and he liked the experience of going around the shelves with her, helping her find what she wanted, because he knew where everything was. He became disoriented and ashamed when there was a reorganisation of the shelving and some goods were moved to a different part of the shop, so that he could not find them with the same certainty and confidence. He hid his shame behind an explosion of anger with 'the stupid people who move things around for no reason at all, just making it difficult to plan how you will shop'.

In terms of communication, Philip usually reported good relations with his parents. They seemed to say little to him. Mostly they watched television programmes together; this worked well as they all had similar tastes. Philip had very definite attachments to certain television series, which for him were very important. Sometimes he seemed to follow the life of the series as a way of living vicariously. This helped to mitigate his fear of not knowing how to conduct himself. With no responsibility in what was shown, he could simply watch the performances and perhaps learn how human life is lived.

Autistic anxiety arises from the fear of unpredictability. Most infants are alarmed by something new, especially if it is sudden like a loud noise. But if children are well and lovingly held, they will learn not to be so frightened unless there are clear dangers. Autistic children and adults may not be easily able to follow that developmental path.

The psychoanalyst Phil Mollon has written about the way in which he understands fear in autistic people. 'A state of not knowing or of uncertainty can be highly aversive for people on the autistic spectrum and can sometimes provoke an illusory confabulated certainty' (Mollon 2015: 173). He traces the fear back to an infant's experience of separation and lack in the early relationship with his mother. There need not have been cruelty or excessive abandonment but the child felt that there was. From then he might well seek solid objects like little toys that will not change and whose permanence he can feel in his hand.

One of the main responses of the rest of the world has been to treat autism as a disease, or at least a psychological syndrome, and to ask

'What causes it?' This is usually intended well and in the case of parents has good reason. No-one would want her child to go through the agony of severe autism, with its rage, frustration and isolation: if a parent knew the cause they might be able to alter it and therefore the discomfort it causes. Yet it seems to be a misleading question. So far, there is no evidence to suggest any kind of psychological causation by cold, unloving parents or by any external impingements like vaccination. Yet, while questions about the origin of autism may be natural and understandable, they have caused severe and lasting damage. Some children have died because their parents have believed the false theory that autism can be caused by the vaccination against measles, mumps and rubella (MMR) and therefore they have refused their child this protection from disease.

Although this belief is totally refuted now, and therefore cannot be said to be relevant to a study of autism itself, it certainly relates to the dangers of unfounded convictions. In this case, it took time to dislodge the proposition made by Andrew Wakefield. Parents wanted and still do want there to be a clear cause for autism that they could recognise and avoid. Andrew Wakefield was exposed by Brian Deer, an investigative journalist writing in the Sunday Times newspaper in the UK. Deer's allegation that Wakefield's conclusions were untrue was upheld by *The Lancet* which retracted the article by Wakefield that they had published and made it clear that Wakefield's research was not trustworthy (Dyer 2010). Wakefield to this day does not accept that he was wrong or misleading. Neil Cameron, a historian who specialises in the history of science, writing for the *Montreal Gazette*, labelled the controversy a 'failure of journalism' that resulted in unnecessary deaths, saying that *The Lancet* should not have published a study based on 'statistically meaningless results' from only 12 cases and that the press should not have given it such emphasis. Wakefield, who believed in this theory, became so convinced that he was right that he attempted to make his data fit his theory. He was not open to conviction that the facts did not support it, even after the exposure by Brian Deer.

Because there is no clear competing psychological or physiological account for the origin of autism, Wakefield's false narrative has taken hold in the popular mind. It is still held by some groups as a narrative that could be called fundamentalist, considering its element of belief and the impossibility of changing it in the face of evidence, such as meta-studies based on sample sizes of millions, which offer no evidence for a connection between autism and the MMR vaccine.

Neuroscience is not able to tell us what causes autism. It is closer to being able to describe the differences in brain function between those with autistic functioning and those with normal functioning known as 'neurotypicals'. Cambridge scientists have established the different levels of connectivity between areas of the brain during different kinds of mental activity. The team led by Simon Baron-Cohen (Baron-Cohen et al. 2000:

355) asserts the importance of the amygdala in animals for normal brain function. He is clear that there is a genetic component to the differences in human brain function. Courchesne and Pierce (2011) have established that in autism there is hyper-connectivity in the pre-frontal cortex and lower connectivity to other systems:

> Connectivity within the frontal lobe is excessive, disorganised and inadequately selective, whereas connectivity between the frontal cortex and other systems is poorly synchronized and weakly responsive and information is impoverished.
>
> (2011: 205)

Blackstock (1978) found that, when listening to music and speech, autistic children give preference to the left ear, which connects to the right hemisphere of the brain. This side of the brain is more involved with vision than the left. This preference would make some sense of the phenomenon that autistic children and adults tend to think in more visual terms than others. Current neurobiological understanding of autism is still developing. There are many other ongoing areas of study that have not yet reached a firm conclusion.

The effect of an imbalance either in terms of hemisphere or connectivity could be that the integrating function of the frontal lobes is impaired, as there is a lack of guidance and control to lower level systems. This would affect executive function and social cognition, which we certainly see in autistic spectrum functioning. There is some evidence of differences in brain structure. Courchesne and Pierce (2011) found evidence of abnormal brain growth in younger cases and abnormally slow growth in older people. What is clear is that the findings so far indicate a disorganised communication within the brain which indicates a high level of anxiety and a need for the establishment of certainties.

Research continues to seek understanding of the connectivity and functioning of the two hemispheres of the brain, and of the amygdala and pre-frontal cortex. Moving on from those initial discoveries, neurologists have continued to look at the connectivity in the brains of people with differing levels of autism and found some differences that do at least begin to describe the situation. This work is still very much at the beginning and the causal chain in conditions that gives rise to autism is still unknown.

From the point of view of someone on the autistic spectrum, the rest of us are noisy, unpredictable and careless of detail, while ignoring the decent requirements of personal space. 'Autism Speaks' is an autism advocacy group in the United States. This organisation and others have been very concerned that autistic people should be respected, and not treated as a group of disabled people. This means that the benefits of autism should be recognised, but also that no-one should doubt that there are very difficult conditions to be faced by those who are more severely affected, who are not functioning well and may remain non-verbal.

The benefits of the high-functioning autistic brain appear to the rest of us in the spheres of cognitive ability, artistic ability, problem solving and attention to detail. These abilities might enable an affinity with, for example, artificial intelligence. As a talent to be exploited, these abilities account for the prevalence of people on the autistic spectrum in mathematics, science and engineering. Taking each of these areas will enable the consideration of the problems as well as the benefits that each can bring and will enable a discussion of the extent to which forms of talking therapy can be useful. High-functioning Asperger's syndrome people will be the ones most likely to seek talking therapies.

Cognitive ability

In the film *Rain Man* (directed by Barry Levinson, 1988), the main character discovers that he has an autistic brother (played by Dustin Hoffman), who has been put into a home to save the family from embarrassment. He is a grown man shown to have exceptional abilities. He can tell the day of the week of any date in the past that is mentioned to him. More importantly in the film, he can remember the cards that have been played in a gambling game and use this information to skew the odds of winning away from the bank in a casino, which provides the brother with opportunities for enrichment. These skills may not be very helpful in ordinary settings but they point to a phenomenal memory and attention to detail, both of which can be very valuable. Although this is clearly a fictional account, it has raised public awareness that some autistic abilities can be positive and that the autistic person can be loved and loving.

Philip (p. 102) is also a man with great potential. He developed the scenarios for some digital games, showing great imagination and innovation. Because he thinks visually, he can see what use could be made of his ideas on the screen. In doing that, he was of great value to his employers but he could not bear the impingements of his fellow workers. He believed that he was disliked by them and that therefore he could never show his true feelings. In therapy he would describe situations in which he found colleagues' behaviour unbearable, but would not know how he could say anything because he knew that his 'interpersonal skills were not good'. Nevertheless, these sorts of creative abilities are one of the great advantages that adults with Asperger's might hold. Some have the ability to remember and draw complicated buildings in great detail. At a fairly ordinary level, this sort of ability to visualise has numerous applications in design and in all kinds of draughtsmanship.

Philip demonstrated intense interest in his online games. He would play games developed by other people in order to see how they worked.

Generally, he found them poorly developed. He was able to remember and describe every detail of the episodes of a game that he was playing. The therapist found it boring and had difficulty in staying awake during these monologues. One day Philip said 'I don't think you like hearing about these games'. This was a great step forwards, as the Philip at the start of the process would never have understood what was going on in another's mind and could not have challenged anyone in such a calm way and might have been uncontrollably angry. The therapist was being invited to show the reaction of intolerance that many Asperger's people have come to expect. She was able to say that she found the level of detail difficult to follow and that perhaps other people were not as interested as Philip was. She was working to enable Philip to feel less shamed and also to understand the reasons for other people's responses to his behaviour. At the same time, she was loosening his damaging conviction that other people would always judge him harshly.

Exceptional abilities can lead to other difficulties. Neurotypical people may expect wonders of a person with this diagnosis and try to make him into some sort of magical stage performer. This leads to a widening gulf, because the person with Asperger's has the conviction that his own view of the world is the correct one and that the rest of the population is careless and superficial and does not understand what is important.

Simon Baron-Cohen (2008) in his book on autism and Asperger's syndrome describes Andrew, a young man who has striking cognitive ability. Andrew's relationship to his teachers is difficult because he considers that they do not research a subject thoroughly. He became interested in the 1944 Battle of Monte Cassino. The rest of the class spent a little time on it and then moved on to another subject. Andrew was unwilling to let the subject go, at what he found a very superficial level. He wanted to know everything about it, including such details as the names of the soldiers who fought there and what happened to each one. As there were a quarter of a million participants and tens of thousands of casualties, the teacher was never going to be able to supply this information. Andrew dismissed the teaching as hopelessly inadequate and superficial.

Andrew's relationship with his teacher was not the only one that suffered from this episode. He was bullied by fellow students and regarded as obsessional. His defence was to think of himself as superior. In the end that led him to study six subjects at an advanced level in one year (the norm would be two to four). He passed all the subjects. Such an ability is impressive, but it does not lead to satisfactory relationships with other young people.

Graeme Simsion (2013) describes in a novel the social difficulties of an autistic-spectrum man who works in a university department. He shows us many of the features of the autistic problem, but does so in a way that invites empathy and admiration rather than mockery.

Don Tilman is a Professor of Genetics and is a very high-functioning autistic man. He has a good friend Gene, who is a professor of psychology, and Don recognises that Gene has a level of social skills way beyond his own. Don has always believed that he would not be able to marry because of his diagnosis and his awkwardness. A well-meaning woman tells him that he could marry and he sets out on what he calls The Wife Project. In the first few pages of the novel we are shown how he embarks on the completely rational course of developing a questionnaire to find a woman who is a good match for him. He depends on Gene for advice but shows his lack of awareness of messages conveyed beyond the surface of words by interrupting Gene's lecture at five o'clock when it was scheduled to be finished even though he sees the Dean of the University there continuing the discussion with some possible funders. He walks in and tells everyone that it is time to stop because he has an appointment with Gene. The Dean says ironically to him, 'Sorry to hold up your meeting, Professor Tillman. I'm sure we can find the money elsewhere'. Instead of recognising the irony, his response is, 'This was good to hear'. In that one moment, Simsion shows the pitfalls that a literal understanding of people's words present to people with this mind-set. But Don is not at all without feelings. He is in fact generous and sets out to help the woman he has met even though he is sure that she will not be a suitable candidate for The Wife Project.

Patterns and repetition

The certainty of knowing all there is to know about a subject gives some sense of safety to a person like Philip or Andrew. No-one can creep up behind him with a new question or piece of knowledge. What he cannot preclude is the use of figures of speech such as metaphors. He arms himself with detail because it leaves him certain and protected. The characteristic forms of repetitive patterns include strong attachments to particular interests like that of Andrew.

This is noticeably different from the way a neurotypical person approaches a subject of interest. An Asperger's patient might be interested in, for example, the work of an important historian, as might any one of a number of people interested in history, but he is not just 'interested'. The Asperger's patient knows the content of all the historian's work, and his life story. Because the person with this kind of brain has often a retentive memory and unusual powers of assimilation and concentration, ordinary (neurotypical) people can find this daunting. Nevertheless, it is an exaggerated form of the behaviour of many ordinary people and so is understood and generally accepted without much difficulty. It is also very valuable in a number of fields to have such memory and such perseverance.

Patterns

More specialised is the love of patterns and therefore of repetition. Frances Tustin (1987) explored the use of patterns and repetition in mental life, including that of people who are not diagnosed as autistic. For children, and even some adults who are autistic, she describes the importance of shapes that can be felt in the body, for example, smearing faeces on the skin, which allows the sensation of the shape of the body. Spinning round and round is also a way of relating a shape to the body.

Clearly, we have to try to understand the inner workings of the mind of a person who has these exceptional abilities and their concomitant anxieties. Why would shapes be important? Shapes form an external predictability that soothes the frightening internal doubts of the earliest experience. An attachment to hard shapes that can be relied on to stay and not change is a characteristic of children and adults who fear the absence of what is needed for survival. Hyper-awareness of shape is not one of the most difficult characteristics and can lead to an aesthetic appreciation of shape and structure. If the infantile terror can be understood and managed, this awareness can also be a strength enabling the sense of design and the importance of colour to lead to artistic creation. This possibility needs to be understood and developed in the face of the difficulty in finishing a project.

Impingement

Anne is a woman who has an autistic-spectrum diagnosis. She has recently discovered that she likes writing science fiction. She can visualise alien landscapes and invent plots, but she says that she gets into great difficulties imagining people, their thoughts and their words. At school she had been told that she had no imagination. On the other hand, she talks at length over the problems she has with the woman next door, whom she describes as 'thoughtless and senseless'. The woman lets her cat come into Anne's house and does not understand at all what an intrusion this is. The therapist points out that Anne seems well able to represent the neighbour very clearly and can make her come alive to the therapist. Anne is surprised at this and says, 'But that's different, that's real'. The therapist merely says, 'All writers have to use what they have experienced, although they may choose to alter it in some ways in fiction'.

Anne seems struck by this. She brings into a session a page on which she has described a person she knows and re-presented him as an extra-terrestrial alien. The therapist is a bit worried about this kind of identity theft and encourages Anne to use her considerable cognitive ability to disguise the identity of the person. Anne understands the practical reasons for this and goes away to work on it. She is a very high-functioning person on this spectrum, with a responsible job, and yet she was still inclined to end her efforts at creativity because she had acquired the conviction that she was no good at imagining.

Autistic shapes are unique to each person. Making shapes brings order and control to the chaos of sensations and experiences that the world offers. Every child has to learn to tolerate this and to wait until she can make some sense of it. For some children with great sensitivity and with some circumstances, such as a depressed or hostile mother, the inner capacity to tolerate uncertainty is not available. Frances Tustin (1987) has given us ways to think about autism in children and has described a three-year-old child, John, who was mute. His first words after a year in therapy were, 'Gone. Broken. Oh dear'. A depressed mother cannot help her infant to separate and in fact cannot help her infant to connect in the first place. John said 'the red button grows on the breast'. Tustin understood that the child was trying to deal with the knowledge that he did not control his mother's nipple and that it had been taken from him in a catastrophic way (1987: 406).

The terror of 'gone'

Innes-Smith (1987) addresses the aetiology or origin of autism in the pre-Oedipal phase as the child's attempt to deal with the terror of separation. He describes it in an adult patient as leading a man to be unable to choose between two women. This is a problem that people often find intractable as long as two potential relationships remain available to them. The difficulty might indicate that the fear is kept at bay as long as the two possibilities are both still present. When a choice is made of one woman, the other possibility is lost and there is no alternative to the autistic terror of 'gone'. Innes-Smith (1987) addresses the aetiology of autism in the pre-Oedipal phase as the child's attempt to deal with the terror of separation. He describes it in an adult patient, a man unable to choose between two women.

The patient was single (divorced) and he had developed relationships with two different women. He described himself as being 'between the two'. This situation resulted in a constant state of tension and anxiety. Each woman knew of the other's existence and he was always compulsively occupied in manipulating the two relationships in such a way that neither woman would break away from him. This situation preoccupied him to such an extent that he could not enjoy the company of either for any length of time. He had to rush off from the one, even in the middle of some activity, in order to see the other, as if to repair the damage which he feared he was doing by not being with her. This was not a new situation to him, for he recalled three different occasions in his life when he had inhabited in this anxious and painful way the space between two women

(Innes-Smith 1987). This difficulty of choosing is not unusual and Innes-Smith relates it to an autistic area of functioning in which the certainty of loss is unbearable.

Not surprisingly, Innes-Smith's patient had experienced difficulty with his own development. He had lived through the last war with his mother while his father was absent. At some level he seemed to be preoccupied by keeping hold of two people who could not be together, both of whom he wanted to keep in a relationship with him. Innes-Smith points out that this man seemed never to have been able to go through any of the more usual experiences of rivalry and anger with his father and love and possession of his mother.

We can at once see that the Oedipal position, when attained, puts the child in the position of choosing between the mother and father and brings with it the threat of losing either or both if a choice is made. This is a problem that patients often find intractable, as long as two potential relationships remain available to them. The difficulty in choosing might indicate that the fear is kept at bay as long as the two possibilities are both still present. If a choice is made, the patient is left with no alternative to the autistic terror of 'gone'. While this difficulty might be more extreme in autistic spectrum adults it is by no means unusual. People may be helped by simply pointing out that this, like other problems, is common to humanity. It can be seen as joining someone to the rest of humanity, not separating him in some shameful enclave of his own.

A child seeks the certainty of his mother's continued existence to fulfil his needs. But according to Phil Mollon (2015) there is a deficiency in autism of some of the essential neurotransmitters for registering pleasure. If Mollon is right, the infant will receive the necessary food from the breast but will not achieve the state of bliss and contentment that we see for babies where this is not a problem:

> If the infant is deficient in neurotransmitters such as dopamine, sero-tonin and norepinephrine, he or she will not find feeding and other interactions with the mother pleasurable or fully engaging.
>
> (2015: 113)

An infant's experience like this sometimes leads to a conviction that the mother withheld something essential and that in turn leads to aggression and/or depression. This is the area of 'normal autism', a stage that every infant goes through in which there is no-one outside of himself but everything is part of him: his sensations and perceptions are all that there is. The child has to pass from the sensation-dominated world of normal autism to what Tustin (1984) has called 'a working relationship with objects in the outer world which can be shared by other people' (1980: 410). It seems that this movement can be deeply conflicted and may be the source of enormous suffering, linked as it is not only to separation anxiety but also to the more primitive terrors of separateness, often experienced in bodily sensation or a physical symptom.

What can help?

Hard objects are reassuring – a child holding a toy car has its shape in his hand. Tustin points out that an autistic child does not play with it in the usual sense but he is reassured by its solidity.

> They [toys] have a bizarre and ritualistic quality and the child has a rigidly intense preoccupation with them, which is not a feature of fantasy play.
>
> (Tustin 1980: 27)

Since autism is about a search for certainty, one of the diagnostic features is an attachment to routines and a hatred of surprises. One of the main difficulties in communication is the need for people to say what they mean. The autistic position involves a dislike, sometimes a hatred of metaphor, irony or hints of any sort that are less than explicit. The autistic person frequently pleads, 'Why can't people say what they mean?'. All these characteristics are important for a therapist to bear in mind. Any comments that she makes work better if they are straightforward and not too enigmatic. A neurotypical may take an enigmatic comment away at the end of a session and ponder its meaning, but an Asperger's patient may find it frightening or exasperating to the extent that he will not return.

Anne Alvarez (1980) describes a patient who began to be able to make use of metaphor. While she was very careful not to let it become a deadening ritual in itself, she was able to help him to form his own metaphors. Gradually, however, it became clear that he had begun to stick to what had been a previously lively image:

> in the same cloying, rigid way as he had with so many physical objects and rituals in the past. He began to use it not to go forward, but to stay where he was and to ensure that I did so too. We simply could not get off the train.
>
> (Alvarez 1980: 71)

Alvarez is pointing out that helping a person with these problems to understand and even use symbolic language needs to be done with awareness of the tendency to fit it into the existing autistic patterns. Instead it needs to be part of a new use of language and from there a new ability to make relationships. She understood that, if an Asperger's patient let go of an idea in one form, they were not always free to develop new versions.

They could be left with the fear of unbearable loss. For the autistic patient, the therapist needs to be the one who understands, including understanding that she must not know too much. The therapist who knows too much will be alarming for most people. The therapist will have to work long and hard to show the patient that it is not dangerous to him but can in fact help him.

Being nothing

Autistic children show us that, in fleeting moments of excruciating awareness, they feel that they are 'nothings' surrounded by 'nothingness'. Lacking the feeling of being held firmly in the encircling embrace of caring attention, interest and concern, they have reacted to such threats by surrounding themselves with soft sensation shapes, and by holding on to hard sensation objects. But these inanimate artefacts are both too hard and too soft. These children need the firm resilience of a human being, whose appropriate and sensible responses enable on-going transformations to take place. Also, it is a truism to say that to be able to play, babies need to be played with.

Talking to autistic people

Since autistic people have difficulties with interpreting both verbal and non-verbal language like gestures or tone of voice, they wish people would always mean exactly what they say. They may find it difficult to use or understand facial expressions, tone of voice or jokes as well as sarcasm. Yet, all language is symbolism and our ability to talk depends on our ability to conjure up in words what is not actually present.

Autistic children are sometimes very slow in learning to speak and may speak very little. This is not through lack of intelligence but is part of an inability to use a code that takes what is not there and elaborates it in some way. The average adult's active vocabulary consists of about 20,000 words with a passive or understood vocabulary of 40,000 words. This implies an immense capacity in neurotypicals to symbolise.

Therapists perhaps have to guard against their own tendency to too much certainty. I have heard supervisees say that this or that patient 'cannot symbolise'. That they have difficulty may not be in doubt but that is not a reason to assume that the process is impossible for them. Someone who can speak of something not in the room is symbolising.

The original process of learning to speak is associated with love and loss. Freud noticed that his 18-month-old grandson was repeatedly throwing a cotton reel out of his cot, exclaiming, 'Oo' as he did so. His actions led to his mother retrieving it for him, at which he would utter an appreciative, 'Ah'. Freud interpreted these babyish noises as *'fort'*, meaning 'gone', and *'da'*, meaning 'there'. Freud discussed the significance of the game in *Beyond the Pleasure Principle* (Freud 1920), suggesting that it shows the child transforming an unhappy situation into a happy one: the lost toy has been retrieved and the mother has responded to a summons. Fairy tales do exactly this when danger is faced and overcome. The Big Bad Wolf nearly, but not quite, eats Red Riding Hood. However, autistic children experience loss as disaster and show us a desperate need to experience recovery and reassurance.

The therapist provides a pattern

In the time and the place of sessions and we try to be as reliable as we can be to hold the pattern steady. This much certainty is possible but cannot be guaranteed. Given that we work only with words and do not play with our adult patients in any literal sense, the task of the therapist is clearly to find ways of expressing the patient's suffering in words. The words will have to relate at some points to the original distress over the deprivation of the mother's nipple, when the baby discovered that it was not under his control but could be taken away and lost to him. If we believe that language is the key to thinking and that thinking is the royal road to the ability to process experience in ways that are helpful and constructive, we will see our work as an attempt to enable patients to see themselves as people with all sorts of abilities. These will include the ability to love and be loved but also to be unashamedly different. In order to achieve that, therapists use every possible opening for communication in the session. We can never allow the dead weight of an old pattern or routine to predominate. Instead we try to express in words the needs and demands and especially the fears of each individual:

> Often, of course, it is the patient himself who gives us the clue. Recently, after a particularly long, defensive discourse, a patient said: 'I feel as I talk that I am reading the pages of a gigantic book. I can even feel the saliva on my finger as I turn the page ...' I said that maybe rather than telling me all these impressive things written in the great book, he just wanted me to know about the feeling of having his finger in his mouth.
>
> (Innes-Smith 1987: 412)

References

Alvarez, A. (1980) 'Two regenerative situations in autism: reclamation and becoming vertebrate' *Journal of Child Psychotherapy* 6(1): 69–80.

Baron-Cohen, S. (2008) *Autism and Asperger's Syndrome.* Oxford: Oxford University Press.

Baron-Cohen, S., Ring, H.A., Bullmore, E.T., Wheelwright, S., Ashwin, C., & Williams, S.C. (2000) 'The amygdala theory of autism' *Neuroscience & Biobehavioral Reviews* 24(3): 355–364.

Blackstock, E.G. (1978) 'Cerebral asymmetry and the development of early infantile autism' *Journal of Autism and Child Schizophrenia* 8(3): 339–353.

Courchesne, E. & Pierce, K. (2011) 'Why the frontal cortex in autism might be talking only to itself; local over-connectivity but long-distance disconnection' *Current Opinion in Neurobiology* 15(2): 225–230.

Diagnostic and Statistical Manual (DSM V). (2018) *Neuroscience & Biobehavioral Reviews* 24(3): 355–364.

Dyer, C. (2010) 'Lancet retracts Wakefield's MMR paper' *British Medical Journal* 340: c696.

Freud, S. (1920) 'Beyond the pleasure principle' in Strachey, J. (Ed.) (1950) SE, Volume XVIII (1920–1922). *Beyond the Pleasure Principle, Group Psychology and Other Works* (pp. 1–64). London: Hogarth Press.

Innes-Smith, J. (1987) 'Pre-oedipal identification and the cathexis of autistic objects in the aetiology of adult psychopathology' *International Journal of Psychoanalysis* 68: 405–413.

Mollon, P. (2015) *The Disintegrating Self: Psychotherapy with Adult ADHD, Autistic Spectrum, and Somato-psychic Disorders.* London: Karnac.

Simsion, G. (2013) *The Rosie Project.* Harmondsworth: Penguin.

Tustin, F. (1980) 'Autistic objects' *International Review of Psycho-Analysis* 7: 27–39.

Tustin, F. (1984) 'Autistic shapes' *International Review of Psycho-Analysis* 11: 279–290.

Tustin, F. (1987) *Autistic Barriers in Neurotic Patients.* London: Routledge.

Chapter 8

Certainty and doubt in balance

If a man begin with certainties he shall end in doubts, but if he will be content to begin with doubts, he shall end in certainties.

Francis Bacon, *The Advancement of Learning*, 1605

Francis Bacon weighed the merits of doubt and certainty and found the value of doubt but only if it can lead to enough certainty to manage life. Psychoanalysis has brought us a way of studying the meaning of behaviour. The framework of intensive meetings over a long period of time enables two people to pay attention to reasons for behaviour that a person might find puzzling. The means for exploring this are provided by the therapist paying close attention to one person's thoughts through good times and bad times, excitement and boredom, love and hate. Something will be gained just by experiencing these feelings in a specialised environment but the main learning is expected to come from the therapist's experience and understanding. She conveys this through all sorts of communication but mainly through her words. One of the main variables in the work of analytic therapists is the way that they make interpretations and what they choose to interpret. The subject of hermeneutics is vast and complex and has been discussed with great energy in all the humanities since Aristotle's interpretation.

What psychoanalysis since Freud has brought to the discussion is a deepening of the questions about consciousness. To what extent is the therapist able to present the patient with an alternative to the conscious convictions that he is showing? Does changing this just mean presenting alternative convictions? Does change depend on the authority that the therapist has acquired in the patient's mind transferentially? Freud noted the potential for 'heads I win, tails you lose' in the therapist's conviction that she has the answer. If the patient accepts the interpretation, it is right; but if the patient refuses it, she merely puts the refusal down to resistance and does not retreat from her position.

In his paper on 'Construction' of 1937, Freud put forwards a view that the therapist is helping the patient to remember what has been forgotten. If the therapist is wrong, Freud did not think it would do much harm. If she realises that she has made a mistake she should say so and will not forfeit her authority. 'The danger of our leading a patient astray by suggestion, by persuading him to accept things which we ourselves believe but which he ought not to, has certainly been enormously exaggerated' (1937: 247). The way in which a therapist can gain some reassurance that she is reading the hints from the unconscious correctly is by listening to responses other than yes or no. Neither of those responses should be taken literally. More useful is a response like, 'I never thought of that before', which indicates that there is some possibility of connecting the conscious mind with the unconscious. For Freud this is all about recovering memories that have been repressed but are accessible. At this point we enter the territory of recovered memories, possibly of abuse, and once again the whole question of the historical validity of memories recovered in analytic therapy is raised. The British False Memory Society claims that families have been destroyed by therapists who became certain that a patient was speaking of abuse that had actually happened and went on to convey that conviction to the patient, in some cases persuading her (usually a woman) to make a complaint at least to her family and maybe to the police. Certainty on the part of the therapist in this context could be damaging as there are many reasons why a patient might bring this narrative to therapy but not be talking of historical fact.

One of the problems brought to light in the early twenty-first century in the UK is the question of whether or not a victim should be believed. There are some therapists who assert that all patients should be believed when they speak of abuse. Why should we think this element of consciousness is more reliable than all the other memories that we might question? The courts have shown that a blanket instruction to police to believe victims' claims of abuse can lead to damaging witch hunts. In the UK and the USA in 2014 to 2019 (the so-called #me-too era), several cases came to light in which people who had made allegations of sexual and physical abuse had been disbelieved from the outset, and the allegations had not been followed up properly. Then, in one notorious case in the UK, numerous serious allegations about historic events were made by a man known as 'Nick', later identified as Carl Beech. He named prominent political figures and celebrities as being responsible. The police publicly declared the allegations 'credible and true' and investigated vigorously. The accusations turned out, after a long period of scrutiny, to be completely untrue – put simply, they were offered up by a man who was described as a 'fantasist', who was later convicted for perverting the course of justice. The investigations and the publicity caused considerable harm to those falsely accused.

False accusations need not be deliberately concocted in order to cause harm. Teachers are particularly susceptible to accusations from pupils. One (male) teacher recounts that in a gender-mixed secondary school class a girl was standing up, shouting at another pupil, causing disorder in the classroom. He went up to her and put his hand on her shoulders to push her back down into her seat. The whole class was witness that it was not at a level of pressure that might have hurt her. The girl, Inez, complained of assault to the Head of the school, who suspended the teacher while the matter was investigated.

Inez was sent to speak to the Student Counsellor, with the expectation that she would help Inez become less disruptive. Gradually she began to talk and told the female Counsellor that her parents were constantly fighting. She added that the fighting was usually just that they shouted at each other. They 'didn't do nothing'. She did however admit that her mother usually came off worse in the shouting matches. 'She would go upstairs and I could hear her, like, crying'. At this point the Counsellor thought that she had enough information to make an interpretation: 'You were angry with your father and you wanted to get your teacher punished because he is a man'. Inez looked pleased. 'That's right. I am really angry with him and I think he deserves to be punished. He really frightens me'. 'Do you worry that your father might hurt you?', asked the Counsellor. Inez hesitated. 'Well, he hasn't yet but he could, couldn't he?'.

The Counsellor took this as confirmation of her theory about the girl's experience and the angry displacement of her fear onto the teacher. In doing so the Counsellor neglected to find out any more about what the reasons for anger with the teacher might be. Instead she went to the Head and told him that she thought that Social Services should be informed and maybe even the police – essentially that an investigation should be launched into the father's behaviour, and indeed the teacher's.

The Head was cautious and unwilling to act without further corroboration. He brought both Inez and the Counsellor in to speak. Inez was horrified. She said that her Dad had never harmed anyone and he just argued with her Mum, 'like anyone's parents'. She wanted to talk about her difficulty in understanding the kind of maths problems that her teacher was currently setting the class. She thought that she was behaving a bit like her Dad shouting at her Mum, because she did not understand the explanations of the problems. 'Perhaps, Dad shouts at Mum because she reads a lot and he doesn't always understand what she's on about'. The problem seemed to be something quite other than what the Counsellor had initially decided – it was an educational issue, not one of abuse by either the father or the teacher. Fortunately, in this case there had not been too much certainty in the Head's mind and the false explanations or interpretations were stopped before they did any harm. This is not always the case.

An important question for all therapists is to decide the basis on which they are arriving at a conclusion that they will hold, even though it might lead to damaging consequences. In the case of Inez, the grounds for the conclusion seem to have been a predisposition to find a reason specific to Inez that would explain her classroom indignation. The Counsellor had a psychodynamic training and had often found that young people were involved with the Oedipal problem of accepting that, when there are two parents, the child has to find a way of loving both of them even if they are fighting with each other. Mechanisms of protection and identification were indeed in play but the Counsellor had stopped with the first possibility that occurred to her instead of turning it round in her mind so that she thought also of the identification with the father in Inez' relations with the teacher. Inadequate or incorrect formulations can be reached for a number of reasons, in particular because of pressure, of whatever kind.

Therapists always have time pressure. They wish to arrive at some sort of conclusion within the 50 minutes of a session. They may also be pressured by external forces, perhaps from their management. Therapists may also be anxious that they will miss a safeguarding need and there may be damage, which they did not prevent and for which they could be blamed. These were the sources of the pressure in the case of Inez, with the school expecting that the Counsellor would help her to fit in to the school structure, and the Counsellor worried about possible future harm to Inez. Patients themselves can exert pressure on a therapist by complaining that they are not helping. Therapists on the whole do not like to take fees or draw a salary that they cannot feel that they are earning. For this reason among many others, they are likely to try to arrive at what looks like an insightful interpretation of what the patient cannot see.

There are many potential reasons that induce a therapist to accept the position of 'the one who is supposed to know'. There may be reasons like the ones above, but a further reason could be to enhance self-respect and the possibility of thinking, 'Yes, I am a good enough therapist'. The potential for harm is one reason to stop and consider the aims of interpretation. Another is the waste of time and money for the patient in going down a misleading path. Many people have the inner strength and intellectual ability to resist an unhelpful comment. On the other hand, the idea that therapy is helping a person to write an autobiography means that many people will not easily reject what sounds like an authoritative statement about what the patient really experienced or intended.

Making meaning

This leads to the question of meaning. Since most people are seeking meaning, is the therapist simply saying that this or that is the meaning of making a false complaint, about something like the action of a teacher, as in Inez's case? Many therapists will consider that a session has gone well if they are able to make a link. They will say perhaps that the patient is angry with her neighbour because the neighbour reminds her of a sister who would never keep quiet when she was doing her homework. This sort of link may be very helpful and may lead the receptive patient to a whole chain of associations and may indeed give sufficient meaning to the present to enable her to make choices.

From the perspective of unsettling the certainties that are harming life in the present, making links is often helpful. The present situation may provide ample reason for being angry, but the past situation to which it is linked adds the thought of another layer of experience distorting the present. Making links is a relatively harmless activity if it stops at suggesting that this or that experience may be similar to something in the past. Yet nearly all analytic interpretations involve making links and may try to impose an intention in the present, which is added to the mere echo of the past in the present. This extra element of intention may involve morality: 'You did this because you wanted to make up for the harm that you thought you had done'. Such an interpretation would be perfectly acceptable in the sense that Melanie Klein's theory of the depressive position (1946) involves wishing to repair the damage, real or imaginary, that the person thinks that he or she has done. Yet, the therapist is adding an element of moral approval through the intention of making amends, which in most societies would be thought to be an acceptable motivation.

Clearly, then, the meaning that emerges will be an artefact of the subject who is listening and finding the meaning in relation with the text provided by the one who is seeking meaning. The text of course is the material brought in the form of memories, dreams, associations and slips of the tongue: all the well-known phenomena of the session. Recognition of this subjectivity is part of what enables a therapist to unsettle damaging certainties and provoke the all-important questioning of established convictions.

For the purpose of considering the part played by conviction in mental life, this book has focused mainly on the convictions of the person involved in seeking meaning. If the discussion were left there, it would perhaps underplay the part of the therapist or other person in the essential process of seeking meaning. In the twentieth century, Martin Heidegger (1927) published his influential *Being and Time*. One of the themes that he addressed is relevant to the hermeneutics of psychoanalysis. If we are interested in Being and what it might mean for any individual, we need to be interested in the one who raises the question. This must apply to the therapist as well as to the person seeking help. Clearly prior thinking affects the therapist in choosing questions to ask and statements of what she understands. This underlies such statements as that quoted by Saks (1999): 'What makes an approach hermeneutic is that it gives some priority to the knowing subject's contribution in constituting and structuring the facts of the matter to be understood' (1999: 5). Saks goes on to consider the position taken by George Klein, that meaning involves understanding intention and that all our work on defence is about intention frustrated, conflicted or denied. (1999: 25). This might be sufficient if the text on which we are working were a matter of agreed facts. The trouble with using a meta-psychological approach is that the 'facts' are, to some extent at least, determined by the expectations and theoretical perspective of the therapist. The whole theory of confirmation bias (see Chapter 3) applies to the therapist armed with her views on the importance of the Oedipus complex or the earlier infantile oral needs.

From all the foregoing considerations we should be able to derive some ideas both about the difficulties caused by the desire for certainty and also some possibilities for alleviating the need and the distress from not being able to achieve it.

One certainty beyond death and taxes

Human life is framed by the certainty that once a woman is pregnant, some process of delivery is inevitable. Many women face this certainty with courage and manage to turn fear into hope, dreaming of cots and little clothes. Women who have given birth before already know what sort of thing awaits them but are still able to face the certainty that they must give birth, perhaps with the knowledge that they survived it before and they might refuse to think about the suffering or they might focus on the joy of the first moments after birth. For men this fear is less vivid and focuses more perhaps on how they will help and what use they can be.

A more conscious certainty is that everyone knows that human life must end in death although of course people differ in how they see that ending and its level of finality. This certainty is often hidden under a layer of hopes and religious beliefs about life after death. Death as a final ending is sometimes evaded by thoughts about dying. Many people will say that they are not afraid of death, but they are afraid of dying. They will go on to think about a better diet or more exercise in order to try to ward off the more painful ways of dying from disease. We all have to accept that there are some certainties but many things remain to be settled in the mind of each individual.

Deflection can help, but also hinder

This brief look at the two certainties of birth and death reminds us that human beings have developed defences against certainties that might trouble us. One aspect of this process is deflection. The pregnant woman dreams of holding her new born baby and does not think too much about the hours of agony that she must endure to achieve it. The possibility of death for mother or baby lurks there too; although that risk is much less in the Western world in the twenty-first century than in the past, it still cannot be ruled out. Yet not many men or women approach the process with the fear of death. At the other end of life, deflection seems to work well. The growth in the uses of medicine develops more clarity about what is within our ability to choose. We believe that we can have a healthier life style and for a long time we can fill our minds with plans to eat less red meat and to walk to work. Hope is also useful as the end of life approaches with inevitability. A woman of 96 said 'something is bound to happen soon', by which she meant that death could not be far away and hope in her case became hope for the peaceful rest, which she had begun to expect of death. She found hope along with Shakespeare's Hamlet in the thought that death is sleep: 'To die: to sleep; no more'.

Can hope provide a certainty?

The second major area that is highlighted here is hope. Hope can be succinctly defined as desirous expectation. The Anglican funeral service speaks of the 'sure and certain hope of resurrection and the life to come'. We may see hope as something to keep a person from depression. It has an honourable place in literature and myth. John Bunyan's *Pilgrim's Progress*, one of English literature's earliest novels (first published in 1678), is an allegory of the journey through life to Heaven. Its protagonist, Christian, meets a companion, Hopeful, who helps him to cross to the Celestial City over a river in which Christian would have drowned had it not been for the help he received from Hopeful. The allegorical meaning is evident in the names. Turning to classical mythology we find the story of Pandora's box. According to Hesiod, Pandora opened a jar which contained all the ills of mankind, such as disease and strife, which then slipped out into the world. She hurriedly closed the jar, but one thing, in Greek named *elpis*, remained trapped inside. This is usually translated as 'hope' but may also be 'deceptive expectation'. Which is the one thing that is not let out? It would be optimistic to think that 'deceptive expectation' was kept back, but pessimistic to believe that 'hope' was withheld from the world. The myth is ambiguous in its meaning. Whatever its original intention, it shows that hope is associated with the ills of human life.

As soon as we turn attention to hope in practice, we can see that it is a complex emotion looking back at experience and forwards to the future. It may be conscious or unconscious. It may have a defensive function in that it can protect from recognition of the suffering in the present. Religions have always built on that function of hope and have given a whole structure to hopes and fears over death and what might follow it. Hope may protect from recognition of the vulnerability and powerlessness of the mortal human being. If it is conscious, it may form a cognitive defence, which expresses the wish for a blissful future.

These functions of hope might be useful but like most human qualities, hope can be excessive and become pathological optimism.

Optimism becomes pathological and fundamentalist when it denies all reasonable doubts and maintains its position unchanged by any contact with history or with reasoned argument. It may damage an individual if it becomes manic and leads into the territory of extravagance and risk taking. Some of the more dangerous new therapies of the last 100 years have offered self-confidence as a cure for anxiety and fear to an extent which, if they were to be successful, would have led to a generation of manically certain, self-confident people. Coming to see a psychoanalytic therapist is in itself a move against pathology but may also reinforce unfounded optimism. The hope is often that the therapist can help to resolve all problems if she only would.

Looking back at the experience of hope that we might all share, we can consider the nature of infantile feeding needs. Any child who achieves adulthood must have been fed several times a day in early infancy. This may be associated with blissful feelings of fulfilment and peace if the baby was allowed to fall asleep in comfort as a result of being full. This, of course, is an image of the fortunate child who has a peaceful and satisfying life in the main. For some, this image may in itself be a wish and not a memory of something that actually happened. It may be known only from other people's descriptions or observation of other babies. This sort of connection may lead to the problems of the overweight adult who attaches hope to an object, particularly food and drink and anticipates feelings of bliss from eating or drinking. Bliss may not necessarily follow: guilt and shame may be the result instead. These feelings lead to a desire to resolve these negative outcomes and to hope for resolution through further eating and drinking. To make use of the hope for the patient's benefit it will be necessary to help to interrupt this cycle. The first problem is to help the patient to understand the process. After that the most difficult problem is the need to relocate the hope into some other process.

Part of the developmental process is learning to accept that desire is not a guarantee of what will happen. Anne Alvarez writes,

> I have looked for a word or concept ... [for] ... the birth and development of hope in a child who may have been clinically depressed all his life. The nearest I can get is ... the 'work of regeneration' or, to paraphrase Daniel Stern and George Herbert, the 'slow momentous discovery that his shrivelled heart can contain greenness'.
>
> (Alvarez 1992: 173)

Even 'hope' can be pathological. Salman Akhtar (1996) has considered the operation of 'excessive hope' and the reason why a person might have to indulge in either hope merging into optimism or despair which develops from pessimism. In the therapeutic relationship hope may develop into the patient's questions about the ownership of the potency represented by the penis or the breast. The therapist is seen as the owner of this potency by virtue of being the 'one who is supposed to know'.

Jacqueline Amati Mehler and Simona Argentieri (1989) described two pieces of work in which the analyst found it necessary to separate herself out from being the one who held all the hope. In the first case, the patient felt hopeless and asked the analyst for some thoughts that would revive hope. The analyst responded internally with some weariness and anger, which most of us would recognise. The analyst recognised her own feelings as counter transference but decided to challenge the inertia and sense of failure. The patient said 'I am afraid there is nothing else to do' and the analyst; decided to respond, straightforwardly and explicitly, 'maybe it's so'. This agreement with a despairing patient shocked her and led to a recognition of the need to make use of the present so that the analysis would not end without being useful. The second patient appeared to be depressed and had reached a position in which he desired to be able to believe that there was no hope at all: 'I can't make it. I can't help it'. To which the analyst said:

> I'm afraid I can't help it either. I'm willing to walk with you up the edge of the abyss and as we have been doing all along, try to see things together but I shall not jump down with you. I will be very sorry indeed if you do... but I shall let you go by yourself ... this is your choice and I cannot prevent it.
>
> (1989: 300)

The patient was silent for a while, as if he had been struck, and later said that he realised for the first time that the analysis could end without him having made use of it. The analyst saw that the time dimension had changed. The hope that the past could be somehow altered was no longer viable. The patient began to realise that it was up to him to make the present into something different. The analyst points out that 'pathological hope cancels realistic hope' (1989: 301).

The time dimension is significant for the therapeutic change that is possible within this sort of fixed certainty. The patient believes that the past cannot be changed so hope is maintained as the only bearable certainty. This might be a necessary stage in analytic work. The past is brought into the room but is found to be whatever at that moment it is. We know that the past changes in memories according to what is happening in the present as well as according to the intervening events. Yet it cannot be changed at that moment nor according to will. What needs to change is therefore a move towards authentic hope, which needs the temporal dimension 'a future time within which for better or for worse, change and transformation can occur' (1989: 300). The past in problematic cases is kept unchanging and is therefore unable to become history.

A patient, Miriam, tells her therapist about a very distressing memory of childhood. Her mother was alcoholic and made her daughter into a kind of slave. Her father had a job which took him abroad some of the time and when he was away there was no-one to intervene on her behalf. She thinks she was about ten when she remembers her mother keeping her away from school. In order to ensure that she would not get out and join the friend who was calling for her, her mother would lock her in her bedroom the night before so that the child could not get out of her room to go to the toilet or the bathroom. She was terrified of the mother, whom she remembered as having a huge red face and a terrible smell of alcohol. Miriam said she could not be sure whether these were memories or whether she had added to them from reading a Victorian children's novel about a girl called Madge whose mother drank gin and treated her very badly. 'Maybe', Miriam said,

> it wasn't as bad as all that but telling you about it doesn't really change it whatever it was. I will always carry the marks of it. I have read enough to know that a mother like that harms the way in which a child develops.

One of Miriam's main difficulties was in her relationships with men. She went to great lengths to let them know that she did not mind them drinking and that even though she did not drink alcohol herself she was 'completely fine' with them drinking. Her most recent relationship had been with Barry. He was an easy-going, sociable man who seemed to like her company, as well as that of other women. She knew that he went out to his Club and met other people including women with whom he had relationships. After a discussion with him, he agreed to stay at home most nights but he liked to sit on the sofa and drink beer. In fact, she found Barry's drinking very difficult and she shut herself away in the room that she called her study in the evening so that she would not smell alcohol on his breath. She had not told him about these memories of her mother and he got tired of spending the evenings alone. Gradually he began to go out to the Club again and sometimes to stay out all night. He apparently interpreted her declarations that she didn't mind what he did as not caring about him. She suspected that he had a lover.

Miriam suffered a great deal from her transference, in which anyone close to her who drank alcohol was a threat to the extent that she was not able to stay in the same room. She was terrified of being locked in by the monstrous image of her drunken mother but she denied that this mattered and she would not accept a connection. She wanted the certainty that it was all in the past and that she could be 'completely fine' with it all. If the therapist dragged up the past, she could not feel that it was left behind. To her, the therapist would be someone trying to lock her in a room with the past. In many sessions she complained that the therapy was not moving on. In other words, she felt locked in. Like the therapist in Amati Mehler's account, the therapist decided that the only way to approach the level of conviction in this transference was to meet it head on. She said,

> I think you want me to join you in the belief that you can leave all the past behind. I believe that we both need to try to understand how it affects you now so that you can have hope of a different experience in the future.

The patient did not like this and did not attend the next session. She did, however, come back to the following session saying that she had thought about it and although she thought the therapist had not really understood her, she was interested in the future.

This vignette demonstrates that the work in the face of this level of conviction is very difficult and the patient's tolerance is stretched very thin so that it might break. It is unrealistic to think that the past can somehow be recovered and changed. Amati Mehler points out that the patient who is trying to achieve this is wanting the same scenario to be replayed in the present. In other words, both patient and therapist are locked into repetition. If the repetition takes the form of repeated complaints and declarations of helplessness it might not be recognised as keeping a past scenario in the present. The therapist needs to see it as such.

One of the areas in which conviction is most important is in the mind of the therapist. There are many ways in which therapists hear recrimination and complaint from their patients. Most will question themselves and wonder whether they are exploiting a patient by continuing with therapy that is not helping. It is essential for the therapist to discuss the issue with her supervisor. This will enable the therapist to consider this aspect reasonably and fairly and sometimes to recognise that she is failing the patient.

On the other hand, one of the most important questions for the therapist is the extent to which she has placed her own hopes on the patient. He is to change, in some probably unspecified way. He is to understand eventually that he owes a great deal to the therapist's patience and understanding. Maybe, in the end, he is to be grateful. At least the patient is to make the therapist into a therapist. His continuing presence will validate her training, her experience and her professional existence.

The therapist's hopes are likely to be non-specific but are based on deep convictions of the value of the work that she does. They are (usually) unspoken but are of the nature of parental expectations: 'I just want you to be happy'. Of course, therapists will not be as crude or as burdensome as this but they may contribute to the patient's hope that the therapist will reinstate the parental figure of the past so that it can be changed, rather than accepting the past for what it was.

Harold Boris points out that the therapist has invested a great deal of hope in her training. She has placed faith in the theory and the theoreticians about whom she has learned and she hopes to have those hopes validated in the experience she has with the patients. On the other hand, the experience is precisely what needs to change. Boris points to the importance of narrative to the therapist. She may be enthralled by the narrative and wish to hear the next instalment. She might well begin to see the therapy as a permanent part of her life, not only for the satisfactions mentioned above and, of course, for the income, but also for the continuation of the narrative. This can be useful if she remembers that the point is not the narrative itself but the fluctuation of the desire behind it. The thought may be, 'What did the patient hope for in telling me that?' Of course, the wishes may be conscious or more often unconscious but they are intricately tied up with hope and, since desires form the bedrock of the unconscious, they need to be always in the therapist's mind (Boris 1976: 150).

Using the metaphor of 'bedrock' to emphasise the certainty of the presence of desire in the unconscious, is a reminder that at every level of the psyche and the therapeutic relationship there are certainties. What lies in the unconscious cannot be changed in Freud's view. However, once it is capable of being put into words, it can be thought, and when it is thought, it could be changed either deliberately or by experience over time. The experience of the therapeutic relationship is in itself of course an experience and can be useful in showing the patient that what seems immutable can be different and have different outcomes. Boris (1976) uses the example of Aesop's fable of the hungry fox who spurns the grapes that he cannot reach as probably sour. That is clearly one possible solution to unfulfilled hope. It has the advantage of being certain. Since the grapes have been removed from reality and now exist only in the sour version in the mind of the fox there can be no doubt about what they are.

As Boris points out, there are other possibilities for the fox. He could have decided that the grapes are not grapes at all but poisonous berries. He could have decided that he is not hungry. Either of these possibilities must be held as a certainty in order for it to remove the sharpness of unmet desire (1976: 147). How is the therapist to address the patient who is using one of these defences? The therapist first gets beyond her own hopes for the patient and can then ask herself what the use of a particular position might be.

Miriam, the patient mentioned above, was experiencing sufficient hope in therapy and the therapist to return to the next session even after expressing her disappointment by missing a session. This missed session is likely to have worried the therapist, who might have thought she had made a mistake in her challenging interpretation. She would need to think about her own wish for the patient to return in order to validate her work. The patient does return and the therapist heaves a sigh of relief. She can rest on her conviction that the patient is deeply attached to her, which means that hope is invested in her, personally. This is useful if the therapist recognises that a process towards living better is the intention of the patient even if unconscious and is able to convey that. Miriam could begin to understand her own wish to be able to change the therapist into a better mother than her own. In other words, the project of understanding has always to include the patient's hopes, so that she will be willing to examine her own certainties when they are used as defences.

Certainty is power

Trying to understand the function of hope as conviction leads further into Freudian theory. Certainty may be experienced as potency. Miriam rejects the therapist's understanding of her situation because it shakes one of her certainties and because it makes the therapist powerful and may make her feel impotent. Such a view means that what is important is not the content of the interpretation but the effect of making it. From the analysis of certainty, the patient can be led to understand something more about the possibility of change, which would not deprive her of her own power. She can of course choose to ignore or deny what is offered to her but she can more usefully see that equating rejection of a threat to her conviction with impotence is not serving her well. The patient can begin to see that rejecting the therapist's interpretations is risking the destruction of her own potential power and is refusing the possibility of being able to make use of the therapist's potency.

Returning to the political thinking of Andrew Samuels mentioned in Chapter 1, we might consider the importance of making the therapist's potency less threatening. He is not an analyst to minimise potency but he does suggest offering more than more than one view of material.

> The political issues are highlighted when the analyst makes his or her uncertainty concerning a multiplicity of viewpoints the central plank of an interpretation. Politically speaking this is far more democratic and likely to lead to dialogue and negotiation.
>
> (1993: 69)

The therapist could take more than one approach to a dream or other material and simply say 'there is this idea and there is that idea and I am not sure which will be more useful now ...' Such willingness not to be certain but to acknowledge doubt without shame is one of the most helpful things that we can do.

Disentangling conviction from potency is therefore an important task in the analysis of distress. It will not necessarily bring about any immediate cure of symptoms but it will assist in the vital project of learning to think, which has to be the main purpose of ending fundamentalism and developing a better life – both internally and in the society in which we live.

References

Akhtar, S. (1996) '"Someday ... " and "If only ... " fantasies: pathological optimism and inordinate nostalgia as related forms of idealization' *Journal of American Psychoanalytic Association* 44: 723–753.

Alvarez, A. (1992). *Live Company*. London: Taylor & Francis.

Amati Mehler, J. & Argentieri, S. (1989) 'Hope and hopelessness: a technical problem?' *International Journal of Psychoanalysis* 70: 295–304.

Bacon, F. (1605) *The Advancement of Learning* (reprinted 1915, by Dent in London, distributed by the Internet Archive).

Boris, H. (1976) 'On hope: its nature and psychotherapy' *International Review of Psycho-Analysis* 3: 139–150.

Bunyan, J. (2003). *The Pilgrim's Progress*. Oxford: Oxford University Press.

Freud, S. (1937) trans. J. Strachey (1938). 'Construction in analysis' *International Journal of Psychoanalysis* 19: 377.

Heidegger, M. (1927) *Sein Und Zeit* (2008) tr Macquarie and Robinson *Being and Time*. New York: Harper Perennial Modern Thought.

Klein, M. (1946) 'Notes on some schizoid mechanisms' in Klein, M. (Ed.), (1984). *Envy and Gratitude* (pp. 1–24). London: The Hogarth Press.

Saks, E. (1999). *Interpreting Interpretation*. New Haven: Yale University Press.

Samuels, A. (1993). *The Political Psyche*. London: Routledge.

Index